体验世界文化之旅阅读文库 **克罗地亚**

Croatia

Culture Smart!

克罗地亚

Irina Ban with David Ronder 著

李奇 注

按照姓氏拼音排序

文库总策划

贾巍巍

文库主编

王守仁 仲伟合

文库副主编

李淑静 石 坚 王 艳 赵 雯

分册主编

仲伟合

高等教育出版社·北京

图字：01-2015-6329号

Culture Smart! Croatia, by Irina Ban with David Ronder, first published by Kuperard Publishing, a publishing imprint of Bravo Ltd.

Cover image:Makarska, on the Dalmatian coast.
Travel Ink/Robin McKelvie
Images on pages 7, 10, 12, 14, 16, 94, 106, 109, 118, 119, 121, and 134 courtesy of the Croatian National Tourist Board
Images on pages 15, 33 © Modzzak; 18 © Georges Jansoone; 19, 120 © Orlovic; 22 © Roberta F. ; 27 © USHMM; 36 © Suradnik; 7, 111 © Nikola Skorić; and 172 © Markus Bernet

图书在版编目（CIP）数据

克罗地亚 : 英文 / (克罗) 伊莉娜·班恩 (Irina Ban) , (克罗) 戴维·朗迪 (David Ronder) 著 ; 仲伟合主编 ; 李奇注. -- 北京 : 高等教育出版社, 2017.3
(体验世界文化之旅阅读文库 / 王守仁, 仲伟合主编)
书名原文: Croatia-Culture Smart!
ISBN 978-7-04-046969-1

Ⅰ. ①克… Ⅱ. ①伊… ②戴… ③仲… ④李… Ⅲ. ①克罗地亚-概况-英文 Ⅳ. ①K954.3

中国版本图书馆CIP数据核字(2016)第318965号

策划编辑	刘　瑾	项目编辑	刘　瑾	责任编辑	周　龙	封面设计	张　楠
版式设计	孙　伟	责任校对	徐艳梅	责任印制	刘思涵		

出版发行	高等教育出版社	网　址	http://www.hep.edu.cn
社　址	北京市西城区德外大街4号		http://www.hep.com.cn
邮政编码	100120	网上订购	http://www.hepmall.com.cn
印　刷	山东鸿君杰文化发展有限公司		http://www.hepmall.com
开　本	880 mm × 1230 mm　1/32		http://www.hepmall.cn
印　张	6.625		
字　数	152 千字	版　次	2017 年 3 月第 1 版
购书热线	010-58581118	印　次	2017 年 3 月第 1 次印刷
咨询电话	400-810-0598	定　价	39.00 元

物 料 号　46969-00

出版说明

为服务“一带一路”国家战略，促进不同文化互鉴共荣，我们引进改编了英国普拉德出版社（Kuperard Publishing）*Culture Smart!* 及 *Simple Guides* 系列丛书，隆重推出“体验世界文化之旅阅读文库”，将带您探索不同的文化，跨越因文化差异造成的交际障碍，领略绚丽多彩的异国风情。

本文库内容涉及五大洲近 100 个国家的独特文化，填补了非欧美等发达国家相关信息缺失的空白。在编排上，同一系列内部采用相同的体例；既可单册阅读，也能满足专题研究和地域文化横向比较的需要。我们约请国内专家团队对文库进行了改编：对疑难词汇、文化现象进行了注释，增加了名人轶事和名校介绍，更新了过时信息；此外，还围绕每个章节的关键事实设计了练习题，以便读者加深记忆和查阅相关信息。

特别要提醒广大读者的是，文化本身属于一个不断发展的范畴。为了增进来自不同文化背景的人们之间的交流和理解，有必要对各国的文化差异进行一定程度的概括，而对文化定势的概括一方面蕴含着准确的文化观察，另一方面也可能出现主观的文化迁移。只有不囿于文化定势，在实践中不断摸索，才能推动跨文化沟通的顺利进行。由于本文库作者的文化背景、观念和个性迥异，他们在描写各国基本国情、历史文化、世俗风情等方面时，难免流露些许个人的偏见，我们本着建立和谐世界的愿望，对一些偏激之言酌情作了处理；我们尊重作者的表达，但作者的某些看法并不代表我们的观点，需要读者予以分析明辨。此外，文库中涉及的有关数据请以中华人民共和国外交部最新公布的数据为准。

就此让心释然，让我们一起体验旅不问人、行随己意的世界文化之旅吧！

高等教育出版社

2017 年 2 月

总 序

在我们这个星球上，有70多亿人口，200多个国家和地区，2,500多个民族，5,000多种语言。在地理位置、历史传统、思想文化等因素的形塑下，人们的生活方式、社会风俗、思维模式、审美情趣、价值观念等呈现出不同特点。在纪念孔子诞辰2,565周年国际学术研讨会上，国家主席习近平指出："不同国家、民族的思想文化各有千秋，只有姹紫嫣红之别而无高低优劣之分。每个国家、每个民族不分强弱、不分大小，其思想文化都应该得到承认和尊重。"

在经济全球化和科技进步的推动下，中国与世界的命运更加紧密地联系在一起。截至2016年3月和我国建交的国家多达173个，随着"一带一路"战略的提出与实施，我国与非英美文化国家的交往日益频繁。在我们大踏步走向世界的过程中，迫切需要了解各个国家的情况，了解各国的人民及其文化。目前国内出版的介绍外国国情的英语书籍大多限于英、美等发达国家，涉及其他国家概况的英语出版物寥寥无几。

为服务"一带一路"国家战略，促进各国人民的人文交流与文明互鉴，高等教育出版社引进英国Kuperard出版社 *Culture Smart!* 及 *Simple Guides* 系列丛书，编辑出版"体验世界文化之旅阅读文库"。本文库共96册，其中亚洲国家28册、欧洲国家31册、美洲国家 16 册、非洲国家 14 册、大洋洲国家 2 册，含“一带一路”沿线国家 45 册；另有一单独画册与科学系列和哲学系列丛书各 2 册。

“体验世界文化之旅阅读文库”用世界的眼光、易懂的语言、深入的剖析为学习者展示出一幅幅多姿多彩的世界各国风情画卷。每册简述相关国家社会文化的基本方面和主要线索，既有关于各国地理、历史、政治、国民性格、信仰、态度和行为习惯的描述，也有对普通人家庭生活、工作和娱乐、饮食特色、商业文化、社交礼仪的介绍。本文库为广大读者提供认识各国社会文化的一把钥匙，为那些准备出国交流、学习、旅游或工作的学习者提供基本的帮助和实用的工具性指南。学习者在阅读的过程中不仅可以知晓相关国家的风土人情，还能了解深层次的文化传统和价值观念，提高对文化差异的敏感度和宽容度，提升跨文化交际的能力。

本文库除国别系列之外，*Culture Smart!* 系列还单独有一画册《世界节日大观》，用 270 幅彩色照片，配以生动的说明文字，呈现世界各地包括巴西里约热内卢的狂欢节和印度阿拉哈巴德的宗教圣节“大壶节”在内的节日瞬间，让读者直观地了解精彩各异的地域文化。*Simple Guides* 系列中，哲学系列丛书展示人类思想发展历史和不同哲学传统；科学系列丛书介绍改变世界的伟大发现和发明创造，能帮助读者加深对我们所生活的世界的认识。

“体验世界文化之旅阅读文库”英语简洁明了，难度适中，语言地道，可供大学生课外阅读。对于英语基础较好、不满足大学英语四、六级水平的非英语专业学生而言，“体验世界文化之旅阅读文库”将不失为习得世界不同国家文化的理想读本。对英语类专业的学生而言，本文库也可拓展学习者的国际视野，增加其跨文化交际知识。尽可能多地接触英语，是学好英语的有效方法，而大量阅读可以培养语感、扩大词汇量、提高理解能力。“体验世界文化之旅阅读文库”可以为广大读者提高英语水平助力。在国家实施“走出去”发展战略之际，“体验世界文化之旅阅读文库”将伴随我们去认识世界、走向世界。

让我们开始体验世界文化之旅，享受英语、享受阅读！

王守仁

2016 年 6 月

分册序

当我们聆听《克罗地亚狂想曲》时，克罗地亚钢琴家马克西姆·姆尔维察用激昂的旋律描述了饱受战争创伤的克罗地亚：空气中弥漫着战火的硝烟，到处是残垣断壁，整个国家都沉浸在一片凄惨悲壮的气氛之中，令人唏嘘不已。然而如今的克罗地亚早已走出战乱，经济逐步复苏，成为了世贸组织一员并于 2013 年正式成为欧盟成员国。但在大多数国人的眼中，克罗地亚仍是一个比较陌生的地中海国家。说起克罗地亚，人们也许只能想起著名的萨格勒布迪纳摩足球俱乐部、杜布罗夫尼克的中世纪古城或联合国教科文组织发布的克罗地亚六大旅游观光胜地。

其实中国与克罗地亚之间的交往和联系源远流长。早在古代，中国的丝绸、瓷器等货物便会途经克罗地亚抵达罗马。此外，对亚欧文化交往起着重要作用的马可·波罗，正是在克罗地亚的科尔丘拉岛（当时归意大利的威尼斯王朝统治）出生。他沿着古丝绸之路来到中国，又通过海上返回威尼斯，打开了中古时代欧洲人的地理视野，在他们面前展示了一片宽阔而富饶的土地、古老而文明的国家，引起了他们对于东方的向往。

建交 20 多年来，中克两国一直交往密切，在政治、经贸和文化等多个领域展开交流与合作。在克罗地亚独立的第二年，即 1992 年，中国政府便承认了克罗地亚共和国，之后两国正式建立外交关系。在 1993 年，克罗地亚总统图季曼对中国进行了国事访问，双方签署了《中克联合声明》，签订了包括《关于鼓励和相互保护投资协定》等多项协定。2015 年 10 月，在中克建立全面伙伴关系 10 周年之际，克罗地亚总统基塔罗维奇女士成功访华，为两国关系发展注入了新的动力。两国元首一致同意，着力挖掘双方各领域合作潜力，提升中克全面合作伙伴关系。而“一带一路”倡议背景下的中国—中东欧“16+1”合作框架，更是为中克两国深化传统友谊、加强互利合作提供了新的合作平台。

那克罗地亚到底是个什么样的国家呢？今天，就让我们跟随着 *Culture Smart*！丛书分册《克罗地亚》，去领略真正的克罗地亚。本书作者伊莉娜·班恩（Irina Ban）是一位对克罗地亚景点、美食和佳酿有着丰富经验的公关代理和顾问，曾多次组织包括《国家地理》《瑞丽》等杂志的记者和摄影师到克罗地亚旅游观光。她深谙克罗地亚旅游业的方方面面，也为克罗地亚与其他国家进行跨文化交流做出了杰出的贡献。在本书中，她从地理、历史、政治、文化、价值观和日常生活等方面，向读者介绍了这个富有魅力的欧洲小国。

和中国一样，克罗地亚也是一个有着悠久历史的国家。早在史前时代起克罗地亚就有人类居住。

铁器时代时古伊利里亚人和古凯尔特人也相继进入。此地区相继经历了罗马帝国时期、独立王国时期、匈牙利时期、哈布斯堡时期以及南斯拉夫时期。不同的时期塑造了丰富多面的克罗地亚文化。

克罗地亚位于欧洲中南部，巴尔干半岛的西北部，地处地中海及巴尔干半岛潘诺尼亚平原的交界处，被誉为“千岛之国”和“度假王国”。克罗地亚北接斯洛文尼亚和匈牙利，东临塞尔维亚，东南连波斯尼亚和黑塞哥维那，南部毗邻黑山共和国；西部与意大利隔着亚得里亚海相望。陆地面积约56,594平方千米。克罗地亚全国设20个省和1个省级直辖市，首都为萨格勒布。克罗地亚的地形多变，西南部和南部为亚得里亚海海岸，岛屿众多，海岸线曲折；中南部为高原和山地，东北部为平原。

克罗地亚深受意大利半岛文化和地中海文化的影响，是中部欧洲文化圈的一部分，有着深厚的文化底蕴。在克罗地亚人眼中，国旗、圣母玛利亚和足球是最为神圣的三样东西，也是最能充分反映克国文化的三样东西。克罗地亚人虽有着斯拉夫民族的开放和地中海国家的风情，但一谈到民族自豪感和祖国时便十分严肃敏感。此外，克罗地亚人在9世纪已基本改信基督教，现国内95%的人为天主教徒。克罗地亚人对足球也十分狂热，位于首都萨格勒布的迪纳摩足球俱乐部更是在各种足球赛事中屡建战功。

克罗地亚人十分地平易近人，爱热闹，擅长运用身体语言来表达情感。这里的人们高大、健硕，非常注重穿着，追求时尚。到过克罗地亚的人对克罗地亚人的热情好客都印象深刻。

相信读罢此书，你可以全面地了解克罗地亚。会发现在这里除了可以观光怡人的海景，还可以释放对足球和时尚的热爱，品尝丰富多样的当地美食。如果您最近计划出游欧洲，不妨跟随这本书的介绍，去探索一下克罗地亚这颗“地中海明珠”，发现更多精彩！

李　奇

2016 年 11 月

Contents

Croatia

Introduction

Croatia is described as "the land of a thousand islands" and "a small country for a great holiday." Most people still remember it as a part of Yugoslavia, and as a country that went to war for independence. Some may have heard only of the medieval town of Dubrovnik, the pearl of the Adriatic and one of six UNESCO sites in Croatia. Others may know that it is short-listed[1] to enter the European Union around 2010[2], or that it is among the world's top ten tourist destinations.

In this small and beautiful country, sea and mountains are within easy reach, and there is a great diversity of landscape, mentality, and life styles. Its rich and turbulent history can be traced back to ancient times, to long before the Greeks and Romans founded their great colonies on the Croatian islands of Hvar[3] and Vis[4].

Culture Smart! Croatia is designed to give you an insight into Croatian values and the Croatian ways of life and work. It looks at how the past has molded the national psyche[5]. A short introduction to Croatian history and language will help you to understand how and why the Croats fought for independence from Yugoslavia, and why this part of the Balkan Peninsula is still one of the most complicated regions in Europe. It will tell you who the Croats are, what are they like, what they respect, how they live and behave, and how you should behave when visiting

1 被列入入围名单
2 克罗地亚是 2013 年正式成为欧盟成员国的
3 赫瓦尔岛，地处克罗地亚沿海达尔马提亚群岛，是沿岸最长的岛屿，靠近斯普利特的南部
4 维斯岛，地处克罗地亚亚得里亚海沿岸，位于达尔马提亚群岛外侧
5 心理

their country. It will guide you through their customs, quirks[1], and etiquette, and offer tips on doing business, communicating, and feeling comfortable with the local people. The Croatian temperament is a mix of Slavic openness and Mediterranean ease, but the people are, not surprisingly, sensitive when it comes to matters of national pride and their state.

Your first impressions may surprise you: you'll notice how cheerful and noisy the Croats are, how they use hands and gestures and touch when they are talking, and their straightforward approach. You will observe that the people tend to be tall and well built, and pay a lot of attention to clothes and appearance, and you may have occasion to remark on the large number of smart cars on the roads in a country where unemployment is running at around 12 percent. Visiting businesspeople are frequently frustrated by the huge amount of paperwork needed to start up a project or get things done, and by lengthy administrative processes. There is one impression, however, that is common to all visitors: that of Croatian warmth and hospitality.

Culture Smart! Croatia offers the first-time visitor vital human information, from background briefings to practical advice on what to expect and how to behave in different situations. By explaining the cultural context behind the dos and don'ts, however, it aims to empower you to discover for yourself the charm, generosity, and humanity of the Croatian people.

[1] 怪异的性格（或行为）

Key Facts

Official Name	Republic of Croatia (Republika Hrvatska)	In 1991 Croatia attained independence from Yugoslavia.
Capital City	Zagreb	Pop. 688,163 (2011 census); incl. suburbs, around 1 million
Other Major Cities	Split, Rijeka, Osijek, Zadar, Pula, Varazdin, Slavonski Brod, Sibenik, Dubrovnik	
Area	87.661 sq.km	Land area, 56.594 sq.km. Sea area, 31.067 sq.km. Number of Islands 1.185 (47 inhabited)
Borders	Slovenia, Hungary, Serbia, Montenegro, Bosnia & Herzegovina; sea border with Italy	
Climate	Continental inland and Mediterranean along the coastline and on the islands	
Currency	Croatian kuna (kn)	
Population	4.284.889 (2011 census)	Birthrate is among the lowest in Europe
Ethnic Make-up	Croats 89.66%, Serbs 4.5%. Other minorities and nationalities 5.84%	
Language	Croatian	Slavic Language, Latin script

Religion	No official state religion. More than 87% of the pop. are Roman Catholic, 4.4% Serbian Orthodox Christian, 1.3% Muslim, less than 1% Jewish, 4% other, 2% atheist	
Government	Parliamentary democracy. The president is head of state, the prime minister head of government.	Elections are held every 4 years for parliament and every 5 years for the office of president.
Media	National TV channels: HTV 1 and HTV 2. Commercial TV stations: RTL and Nova TV. National radio stations: Croatian Radio 1, 2, and 3. Commercial stations incl. Radio 101, Narodni Radio, Otvoreni Radio	**Main dailies are *Vecernji List* and *Jutarnji List*. Main regional dailies are *Slobodna Dalmacija* (Dalmatia) and *Novi List* (Istria). Minor regional papers are *Glas Slavonije* and *Feral Tribune*. Daily tabloid: *24 Sata***
Media: Foreign Language	Foreign-language publications available at kiosks in major cities. No English-language daily for foreigners	Satellite and cable TV available. In summer Radios 1, 2, and 3 broadcast news in English, German and Italian.
Electricity	220 volts, 50 Hz	Standard two-prong plug. US devices require adapters.
Video /TV	PAL B/G, PAL D/K	
Internet Domain	.hr	
Telephone	Country code: 385 Zagreb city code: 1	Put 0 before area code when dialing within the country. To call out, dial 00 plus country code.
Time Zones	Central European Time: GMT + 1	

Chapter 01

LAND & PEOPLE

1 地中海的
2 巴尔干半岛（地处欧洲东南部，位于亚得里亚海和黑海之间，是南欧三大岛之一）
3 萨格勒布（克罗地亚首都，位于克罗地亚的西北部）
4 斯洛文尼亚（前南斯拉夫成员共和国）
5 匈牙利（欧洲中部国家）
6 塞尔维亚（前南斯拉夫成员共和国）
7 波斯尼亚和黑塞哥维亚（前南斯拉夫成员共和国）
8 黑山共和国（前南斯拉夫成员共和国）

A GEOGRAPHICAL OVERVIEW

The Republic of Croatia is both a Middle-European and a Mediterranean[1] country. It is located in Southern Europe and lies partly in the Balkan Peninsula[2]. The capital is Zagreb[3]. Croatia shares land borders with Slovenia[4] and Hungary[5] in the north, Serbia[6] in the east, Bosnia-Herzegovina[7] in the south and east, and Montenegro[8] in the south. There is a sea border with Italy to the west. Its mainland territory is divided in the south by Bosnia-Herzegovina's short coastline (9.315 miles; approximately 15 kilometers).

Croatian territory extends from the furthest

eastern edges of the Alps in the northwest to the Pannonian[1] lowlands and the banks of the Danube[2] in the east; its central region is covered by the Dinara[3] mountain range, and its southern parts extend to the coast of the Adriatic Sea[4]. The mainland covers approximately 21,850 square miles (56,594 sq. km). The highest peak is Mount Dinara, which has an altitude of 6,007 feet (1,831 meters) above sea level.

The Adriatic Sea stretches from the Balkan Peninsula to the Apennine Peninsula[5]. The part belonging to the Republic of Croatia is the east coast, which extends all the way from Prevlaka[6] in the south to Cape Savudrija[7] in the west, including all islands, islets, and cliffs along the coast, and the archipelago[8] of Palagruža[9]. The coastline is

1 潘诺尼亚的（古罗马中欧省份，位于多瑙河和萨瓦河之间）
2 多瑙河（发源于德国，流经奥地利等十个国家，后注入黑海，是欧洲第二大河流）
3 迪纳拉山脉（地处欧洲东南部，为欧洲第四大山脉）
4 亚得里亚海（位于意大利东海岸和巴尔干半岛之间，是地中海的一个大海湾）
5 亚平宁半岛（现大部分在意大利境内，也称意大利半岛；是南欧三大岛之一）
6 普雷夫拉卡岛（现属黑山共和国）
7 皮兰角（位于亚得里亚海的子海湾——皮兰湾域内，靠近斯洛文尼亚的皮兰市）
8 群岛
9 帕拉格鲁扎群岛（克罗地亚境内群岛）

3,625 miles (5,835 km) long, of which 2,521 miles (4,058 km) surround 1,185 islands, solitary rocks, and reefs — but of these only fifty islands are inhabited. The largest islands are Krk[1] and Cres[2], in the Kvarner[3] region.

There are eight protected national parks[4] (Plitivice Lakes, Brijuni, Risnjak, North Velebit, Paklenica, Krka, Kornati, and Mljet), eleven nature parks, and six UNESCO[5]-listed sites.

CLIMATE

There are two climate zones in Croatia: a temperate, continental climate with both snow and sun in the interior, and a pleasant, Mediterranean climate, with an overwhelming number of sunny days, that prevails along the Adriatic coast, giving hot, dry summers and mild, humid winters. Snow is so rare on the coast that on the island of Hvar, which enjoys more sunshine than anywhere else in Croatia, hotels offer free accommodation if snowflakes[6] surprise the guests in January and February.

Inland, the average temperature ranges from

1 克尔克岛（位于克罗地亚境内，地处亚得里亚海北部）
2 茨雷斯岛（位于克罗地亚境内，亚得里亚海沿岸岛屿）
3 克瓦内尔（克瓦内尔海湾是亚得里亚海的一个子海湾，位于亚得里亚海的北部，以克尔克岛和茨雷斯岛为屏障）
4 国家公园（克罗地亚境内共有八座国家公园，依次是普利特维采湖区国家公园、布里俄尼群岛国家公园、里斯尼亚克国家公园、北韦莱比特国家公园、帕克莱尼采国家公园、卡尔卡国家公园、科纳提国家公园和姆列特国家公园）
5 联合国教育、科学及文化组织（联合国教科文组织）的缩写，该国际组织旨在促进各国间的教育、科学和文化的合作；其总部设在法国巴黎丰特努瓦广场，截至 2011 年，共有成员国 195 个，另有九个准成员，共计 204 个国家和地区
6 雪花

32–36°F (0–2°C) in January to 70–82°F (21–28°C) in August. Winters are snowy and fog is common in autumn. Subzero temperatures are possible in December and January. Seaside temperatures average 43–59°F (6–15°C) in January and 77–95°F (25–35°C) in August. The sea temperature is about 54°F (12°C) in winter, and 77–81°F (25–27°C) in summer. At the height of summer, temperatures can reach up to 99°F (37°C) in the shade.

The biggest surprise with Croatian weather could be the humidity—it can be unpleasant in the summer months, particularly inland, where summer winds are rare. By contrast, on the coast there is a welcome west wind (locally known as the *maestral*) that blows during the hottest part of the day (1:00–4:00 p.m.), and brings some relief. The most pleasant seasons to travel and explore Croatia are spring and fall, when it is not so crowded and the climate is at its most comfortable.

POPULATION

Croatia has 4,280,000 inhabitants, according to the most recent census[1], and slightly more women

1 人口普查

than men. The average age of the population is 39.3, which makes Croatia an "old" country, with a life expectancy of 71 for men and 78 for women. About 90 percent of the population are Croats, with Serbs[1] forming the main minority.

Population distribution varies: Zagreb and Zagreb County have the highest density, while Lika[2] and Gorski Kotar[3] and parts of Slavonia are depopulated[4] and close to being a wasteland. In response the state is introducing programs to encourage entrepreneurship[5] and economic initiatives, aiming to create livelihoods for the people there.

Croatia has had a high emigration rate. Substantial and active Croatian communities can be found in the USA, Australia, Germany, and New Zealand, mostly centered on church associations, and many young Croats win scholarships and complete their education abroad.

REGIONS AND CITIES

There are twenty-one counties, divided among the four main regions: Central Croatia; Istria[6] and

1 塞尔维亚人
2 利卡地区，位于克罗地亚中部
3 戈尔斯基科塔尔地区，以山区为主
4 人口减少
5 创业精神
6 伊斯特里亚（欧洲巴尔干半岛西北部的半岛）

the northern seacoast with mountainous Croatia; Slavonia; and Dalmatia[1].

Istria and the northern seacoast with mountainous Croatia consists of the Istrian Peninsula, the Kvarner region (the coastline, with the town of Rijeka[2] as capital, and the islands of Krk, Cres, Lošinj[3], and Rab[4]) and mountainous areas with a low population. The inhabitants of Istria are known for their diligence and stubbornness[5]—a combination of characteristics inherited from their Italian and Austrian neighbors—and their appreciation of a pleasant and comfortable way of life.

Dalmatia is divided into Northern Dalmatia, with Zadar[6] as its main city, Middle Dalmatia, with Split[7], and Southern Dalmatia, with Dubrovnik[8] as its capital. Off the coast of Dalmatia there are three island groups: the North Dalmatian Islands (including the Kornati National Park with 150 islets), the Middle Dalmatian Islands (Hvar, Brač, Šolta, and Vis) and the South Dalmatian Islands (Korčula, Lastovo, the Elafitis, and Mljet). The people here tend to be true hedonists[9]—fonder of

1 达尔马提亚地区，包括亚得里亚海沿岸的达尔马提亚群岛和附近 1,000 多个小岛；总面积 1.3 万平方公里，其行政中心为斯普利特
2 里耶卡市（克罗地亚境内的一座港口城市）
3 洛希尼岛，位于亚德里亚海北部，克瓦内尔湾内
4 拉布岛，位于达尔马提亚最北部分，著名的旅游胜地
5 倔强；顽固
6 扎达尔市（克罗地亚西南部海港）
7 斯普利特市，历史名城；克罗地亚第二大城市，是达尔马提亚地区第一大海港
8 杜布罗夫尼克市（克罗地亚南部港市，濒临亚得里亚海）
9 享乐主义者

1 谷仓，粮仓
2 郊区；市郊
3 “新艺术”建筑，受19世纪末20世纪初的“新艺术”运动的影响，强调自然风格，反对过分装饰风格（如维多利亚风格等）
4 奖励，激励

friendship and pleasure than of money.

Those who inhabit Slavonia, in easternmost Croatia, are said to have souls as open as the wide fields of this fertile region, which is nicknamed "Croatia's granary[1]".

Zagreb

Zagreb, the capital (population 688,163, or about 1 million including the outskirts[2]), was founded in 1242. The economic, cultural, and administrative center of the country, it has Art Nouveau architecture[3] typical of the **Austro-Hungarian Empire**, with characteristic city parks, fountains, and coffee shops along the main streets. Zagreb is the only substantial Meetings, Incentive[4], Congress, and Events center in Croatia, though other cities also have some good facilities.

奥匈帝国 (Austro-Hungarian Empire)

该国于1867年建立。横跨中欧、南欧和东欧，幅员辽阔，在当时国土面积欧洲第二，仅次于俄国，是当时的世界八大列强之一；实行双首都制，在奥地利是维也纳，匈牙利是布达佩斯；该国于1918年解体。

A feature of Zagreb's social life is the "Saturday walk", when everyone who wants to see and be seen dresses in their best and heads for Flowers Square in the city center for coffee and conversation. This social gathering, resembling nothing so much as a catwalk fashion parade, lasts until 1:00 p.m.

Zagreb has a famous football team, Dinamo[1], which has a historic rivalry[2] with Croatia's other famous club, Hajduk ("Pirates") from Split.

Split

Split, with 400,000 inhabitants, is the center of Dalmatia and, apart from Dubrovnik, is the main tourist center on the Croatian coastline. It is the beloved hometown of tennis player Goran Ivanišević[3], who won Wimbledon[4] in 2001. Split has one particularly notable social phenomenon: no matter when you arrive, the streets are alive and the coffee shops full. The city is a perpetual social mingler[5]. Appearances are important here, with designer clothes and a well-toned[6] body *de rigueur*[7]. It may also be useful to know that Split has

1 萨格勒布迪纳摩足球俱乐部，克罗地亚著名足球队，于 1945 年正式成立，主场在原哈斯克的马克西米尔球场；共计获得欧洲联盟杯冠军一次，亚军一次，曾有兹拉特科·克拉尼察、达沃·苏克等明星球员

2 竞争；对抗；竞赛

3 伊万尼塞维奇，克罗地亚著名网球男运动员，1971 年出生于斯普利特，身高 193cm，7 岁便开始打网球，在 2001 年拿下温布尔登男单冠军，现居于蒙特卡罗

4 温布尔登网球锦标赛，网球赛事中最古老的赛事之一，首次比赛于 1877 年举行，现为世界网球四大满贯之一；该比赛于每年的 6–7 月间在英国伦敦郊区温布尔登举行，比赛包括男子单打、女子单打、男子双打、女子双打和男女混合双打比赛等

5 搅拌器

6 线条良好的

7 流行的，时髦的；按习俗（或时尚）所要求的

a reputation as the town with the most beautiful women in Croatia! Central Split also has some historical charm, due to the famous ruins of Diocletian's Palace (c. 305 CE), which is listed as a UNESCO World Heritage Monument.

1 高速公路
2 造船厂
3 生气勃勃的
4 别墅

Rijeka

Rijeka, with 250,000 inhabitants, is situated in the Gulf of Kvarner, just two hours' drive from Zagreb via the new expressway[1]. The town is known for its shipyard[2] and sailing traditions, and also for its exuberant[3] Carnival in February, which was flagged by the London *Times* in 2007 as an unmissable winter destination. During Carnival week the city puts on a different face, giving itself over to music, dancing, and fun. Just to the north of Rijeka lies the Opatija Rivijera, a smart, exclusive, seven-and-a-half-mile (12-km) seaside parade, with villas[4] and expensive private hotels suitable both for weekend relaxation and for business conferences and events. Friday afternoons can be busy on the road to Rijeka.

Osijek

Osijek, in far eastern Slavonia, has 200,000 inhabitants. Known as the greenest city in Croatia, it has an authentically small-town atmosphere: life carries on peacefully and everyone knows everyone else. It has wide avenues, spacious squares, and seventeen parks. Osijek's surroundings offer plenty of day-trip options, including bicycling along the Danube, fishing in the Drava, hunting and hiking in the Kopački Rit Nature Park, or visiting the castles that are all just a short distance from the city. Kopački Rit is considered to be the best birdwatching location in the country.

Dubrovnik

Dubrovnik, with 50,000 inhabitants, is the best-known tourist destination in Croatia. The old city, with its imposing walls, dates from the twelfth century and is a UNESCO World Heritage site. Citizens of Dubrovnik still call it just "The Town", a hangover from the age of the Dubrovnik Republic (from the fourteenth to the seventeenth century), when it maintained a proud independencc from both the Venetian Empire[1] and the Habsburg Crown[2]. The inhabitants still address each other, as they go about their daily lives or meet on the street, as *Gospar*, a local term for "gentleman", because Dubrovnik was an aristocratic[3] republic, with a constitution dating back to 1272, and the old patrician[4] sense persists among its natives. Contemporary Dubrovnik is an expensive place to live, but many foreigners are buying up properties there. In summer the city opens up to the world with the Dubrovnik Summer Festival, a member of the European Festival Association, and the jet set come to town to enjoy its many charms as an upscale[5] vacation resort. To name just a few celebrity visitors, John Malkovich[6] (who is of Croatian origin himself),

1 威尼斯共和国，该国早期隶属于东罗马帝国，于 8 世纪取得自治，在中世纪向亚得里亚海扩张，控制了爱琴海域内的诸多岛屿。后逐渐衰落，1797 年被拿破仑灭亡，最终成为奥地利帝国的一部分

2 哈布斯堡家族，其祖先可追踪至公元六世纪法国的阿尔萨斯公爵，家族势力庞大，繁衍甚广，是欧洲历史上统治领域最广的王室，曾统治神圣罗马帝国、奥地利帝国、奥匈帝国、西班牙帝国等，后衍变为奥地利哈布斯堡王朝、西班牙哈布斯堡王朝和哈布斯堡－洛林皇朝三个分支

3 贵族的；主张贵族政治（或统治）的

4 贵族的

5 迎合高层次消费者的；高档的

6 约翰·马尔科维奇（1953–　），美国男演员、制片、导演和编剧，曾获第 57、66 两届奥斯卡最佳男配角奖，代表作有《推销员之死》和《心田深处》等

Princess Caroline[1] of Monaco, Tom Cruise[2], Sir Roger Moore[3], and Formula One[4]'s Bernie Ecclestone[5] have all stayed in Dubrovnik recently.

A BRIEF HISTORY

Croatian history is marked by a succession of different cultures that have from time to time replaced or blended into each other. Under the **Emperor Constantine**, in the fourth century CE, Croatian territory straddled[6] the border between the Western and Eastern Roman Empire. It stood at the border of the Frankish Empire[7] and Byzantium[8] in the ninth century, of Eastern and Western Christianity in the eleventh century, and on the front line between Christianity and Islam from the fifteenth to the nineteenth century.

1 卡罗琳公主（1957– ），摩纳哥大公主；是前摩纳哥国家元首——兰尼埃三世亲王与摩纳哥王妃——格雷丝·凯莉的长女。是现在位亲王阿尔贝二世的亲姐姐

2 汤姆·克鲁斯（1962– ），美国男演员，电影制片人，曾获第47届和54届金球奖最佳男主角，代表作有《夜访吸血鬼》、《甜心先生》和《碟中谍》等

3 罗杰·摩尔爵士（1927– ），英国男演员，第三任007扮演者，是007扮演者中"年龄最大、任期最长"的邦德

4 一级方程式赛车，是当今世界最高水平的赛车比赛，与奥运会、世界杯足球赛并称为"世界三大体育盛事"；该赛事由国际汽车运动联合会（FIA）举办，采取积分赛制

5 伯尼·埃克莱斯顿（1930– ），F1控股公司的老板，持有F1赛事的商业经营权，被视为"F1赛车帝国的国王"，将F1赛车从最初的混乱不堪、经营惨淡的比赛项目，变成今天这样一个产值数十亿美元的王国

6 跨立于；跨越

7 法兰克王国，5世纪末~10世纪末由日耳曼法兰克人在西欧建立的封建王国，其领土包括今日的法、比、卢、荷、德、奥、瑞士、北意大利及西班牙的边地。现在的捷克同南斯拉夫的地方都是它的附庸国

8 拜占庭（古罗马城市，今称伊斯坦布尔）

君士坦丁大帝 (Emperor Constantine, 272–337)

古罗马帝国统治者，君士坦丁大帝是古罗马第一位信奉基督教的皇帝，他于公元330年迁都至拜占庭，并改名君士坦丁堡；君士坦丁大帝颁布的一系列措施促进欧洲从奴隶社会向封建社会转变，史称"千古一帝"。

1 本土的；土著的
2 摇篮；发源地；发祥地
3 商业的；商人的
4 航海的，海上的
5 古代；古物

Croatia has had many foreign rulers: Italian influence is strong along the coastline, and Hungarian and Austrian manners can still be seen in the continental interior. But there are also proud indigenous[1] traditions going back several centuries. On the island of Hvar, for example, the first public theater was opened in 1612, making it a contemporary of Shakespeare's Globe. It still hosts performances today.

The Adriatic Sea, a gulf of the Mediterranean reaching deep into the continent of Europe, was the cradle[2] of ancient civilizations, and an important mercantile[3] and nautical[4] route in antiquity[5]. The eastern shores were inhabited as early as the beginning of the Stone Age. Painted pottery found at Hvar and in eastern Slavonia dating from 3000 BCE points to an advanced Neolithic[1] culture. In the fourth century BCE the ancient Greeks were trading with the native Illyrians[2] by sea, and they founded colonies on Croatian islands, with settlements at Pharos, today's Starigrad[3], on the island of Hvar, and on Issa, the Latin name for the island of Vis. In the third century BC the Greeks sought Roman help against the Illyrian Queen Teuta[4], and Rome's influence in the area grew.

In the year 9 CE Tiberius[5], heir to the Emperor Augustus[6], annexed[7] the Eastern Adriatic and its hinterland[8]: the coastal region became the Roman province of Dalmatia, while northern and eastern Croatia were absorbed into the provinces of Noricum[9] and Pannonia. The Romans built magnificent palaces and summer residences, most notably on the island of Brijuni and Diocletian's Palace in Split.

In the fifth century CE the Roman Empire succumbed[10] to barbarian[11] invasions. Croatia was invaded by the Ostrogoths[12], and in the sixth century by the Avars[13]. In the seventh century

1 ［古］新石器时代的；
2 伊利里亚人
3 斯塔里格勒（旧称 Pharos），地处克罗地亚达尔马提亚地区斯普利特－达尔马提亚县赫瓦尔岛北侧，历史悠久，是欧洲最古老的城镇之一
4 托伊塔女王，古伊利里亚的女王，生活在公元前 3 世纪晚期，史称“海盗女王”；在她摄政期间，她的舰队掠夺罗马人的财物，射杀并羞辱罗马使节，罗马因此向伊利里亚宣战并赢得胜利；后在第二次马其顿战争中倒向马其顿，罗马和希腊联手从伊利里亚登陆，古伊利里亚就此覆灭
5 提比略（公元前 42 年 12 月 16 日—公元 37 年 3 月 16 日），古罗马第二任皇帝
6 奥古斯都（公元前 63－公元 14），罗马帝国第一代皇帝（公元前 27－公元 14），恺撒的甥孙、养子、继承人，原名屋大维）
7 兼并（领土等），强行占取（领土等）
8 腹地
9 诺里库姆，是古罗马帝国诸行省之一，领土范围大概在今天的奥地利与捷克的部分地区
10 屈服
11 野蛮的；未开化的
12 东哥特人（哥特人的东支，曾于公元 5 世纪在意大利建立东哥特王国
13 阿瓦尔人（现居于高加索地区、操乌拉尔阿尔泰语的人）

[1] 斯拉夫的
[2] 喀尔巴阡山脉的（位于欧洲中部。在多瑙河中游以北。全长 1,450 千米。西起奥地利与斯洛伐克边界多瑙河峡谷，向东呈弧形延伸，经波兰、乌克兰边境至罗马尼亚西南的多瑙河谷的铁门峡谷。）
[3] 公国
[4] 从而，因此

the Croats, a Slavic[1] tribe from north of the Carpathian[2] mountains, arrived in the country.

Croatian Sovereignty

The early Croats were ruled by native-born dukes and kings. They established two principalities[3] upon arrival: Dalmatia on the Adriatic Sea and Pannonia in the east. They accepted Christianity in the seventh century, and for a while successfully played off the Frankish and Byzantine Empires against each other. The first dynasty was the Trpimirovices. In 925 **King Tomislav**, the first Croatian king, united Dalmatia and Pannonia and reorganized the Croatian Church, thereby[4] lessening the Pope's control. This period lasted till 1102, when Croatia entered a dynastic

托米斯拉夫国王 (King Tomislav, 约 880–928)

托米斯拉夫是克罗地亚特尔皮米罗维奇王朝大公 (910–925)，后成为克罗地亚的第一任国王 (925–928)。

union with Hungary on the dying out of the native-born royal male line.

Union with Hungary (1102–1526)

Croatia became part of a new Hungarian-Croatian kingdom united under the same royal family, the Arpads. The document by which the two nations entered this new arrangement is called the Pacta Conventa[1] (1102). However, Croatian institutions soon lost their independence. This situation lasted until the defeat of Hungary by the Ottoman Turks[2] at the **Battle at Mohács** in 1526. The King of Hungary, Louis II[3], who died in battle, was succeeded by the Austrian Ferdinand I[4] of Habsburg. Since the victorious Turks now

1 约定条款，该条约同意让匈牙利国王担任克罗地亚君主，自此克罗地亚即成为匈牙利的一部分

2 奥斯曼土耳其人

3 拉约什二世，弗拉迪斯拉斯二世的继承人，于 1516 年继位，1521 年亲政；是亚盖隆王朝的匈牙利国王和波希米亚国王，1526 年在第一次摩哈赤战役中战死

4 斐迪南一世，托斯卡纳大公（1587 年—1609 年在位），在位期间与奥地利哈布斯堡王朝的统治者们保持良好关系，曾帮助奥地利抵挡奥斯曼帝国的进攻

第一次摩哈赤战役 (Battle at Mohács, 亦称莫哈奇战役)

奥斯曼帝国国王苏丹苏莱曼一世在 1521 年要求匈牙利国王乌拉斯洛二世和其子拉约什二世纳贡，但遭到拒绝；苏丹苏莱曼一世于 1526 年率领土耳其人向匈牙利进军；该战役是匈牙利被土耳其人彻底击败的一次战役，标志匈牙利王国的真正灭亡，并为哈布斯堡和土耳其统治匈牙利铺平道路。

[1] 附庸国；属国
[2] 保护国；摄政政体

occupied a large part of the Hungarian empire, leaving Croatia dangerously exposed, the Croatian parliament accepted the protection offered by the Habsburgs in 1527.

Habsburg Rule (1527–1918)

Apart from the narrow coastal strip controlled by the Venetian Republic, Croatia was now a Habsburg dependency[1]. Gradually the Habsburgs drove the Turks out of central Europe. The coastline and islands remained Venetian until conquered by **Napoleon** in 1797. For a brief period it flourished as a French protectorate[2]—which actively promoted the development of

拿破仑 (Napoleon, 1769–1821)

十九世纪著名军事家、政治家；曾执掌法兰西共和国，后创建法兰西第一帝国；执政期间，多次发动战争向外扩张，五破反法联盟，占领欧洲大片土地，建立了庞大的拿破仑帝国；后于 1815 年滑铁卢战争失败后，被流放至大西洋的圣赫勒拿岛，1821 年在此病逝。

South Slav[1] consciousness—but after Napoleon's defeat in Russia the coastline was annexed by the government in Vienna, in 1813. Croatia as a whole remained part of the Austro-Hungarian Empire until the end of the First World War.

During the mid-nineteenth century, the movement for democratic reform unleashed[2] by the Napoleonic wars swept across Europe.

National consciousness grew in Croatia and led to calls for independence from Hungary and the creation of an autonomous[3] Croatian state within the Habsburg Empire. The man who had the crucial role in this awakening of Croatian national spirit was **Ante Starčević**, the leader of the Party of Rights. The Hungarian government dominated Croatia culturally and exploited it

1 南斯拉夫，以从奥斯曼土耳其帝国独立的塞尔维亚族所建立的塞尔维亚王国为基础，经两次巴尔干战争及第一次世界大战，击败奥斯曼土耳其帝国、奥匈帝国及周边诸小国，吞并原来从属于此二帝国的各弱小民族聚居地而形成的国家
2 发动；解放
3 自治的；自主的

安特·斯塔尔切维奇 (Ante Starčević, 1823–1896)

克罗地亚政治家，被誉为“祖国之父”，克罗地亚民族解放运动领袖，现代克罗地亚国家肇建者。

1 君主政体；君主国
2 （尤指个人或党派间）临时结成的联盟
3 南斯拉夫的
4 分割，瓜分
5 摄政王

economically. In response to the hegemonic policies of the Habsburg monarchy[1], the idea of a united state of Southern Slavs (or Yugo-Slavs) acquired more force. The Serbs, who were outside the monarchy, were in favor of this idea, too, seeing it as a way of enlarging their state, creating a Greater Serbia, and gaining access to the Adriatic Sea. The Croats, on the other hand, saw it as a cultural union of Slavic nations, who would eventually achieve full political autonomy. As a result, in 1905 the Croatians and the Serbs formed a coalition[2] with the aim of creating an independent Yugoslav[3] state.

The Creation of Yugoslavia (1918–41)

After the First World War, Austria-Hungary was dismembered[4]. On December 1, 1918, Croatia became part of the new Kingdom of Serbs, Croats, and Slovenians proclaimed by **Aleksandar Karadordević**, Prince-Regent[5] for his father, Peter I of Serbia, while Istria and the towns of Rijeka and Zadar came under Italian rule. Although carried out in the name of national

亚历山大·卡拉乔尔杰维奇 (Aleksandar Karadordević, 1806–1885)
塞尔维亚大公（1842–1858）。早年在俄军中服役。1842 年被国民议会推举上台以代替被废黜的米哈伊洛·奥布雷诺维奇大公，开始卡拉乔尔杰维奇王朝在塞尔维亚公国的正式统治。对外政策动摇不定，或亲俄或亲奥；在 1848–1849 年革命中，未派军支援匈牙利的斯拉夫人；克里米亚战争中迫于奥、土压力，持中立立场。1858 年 12 月被国民议会废黜，卡拉乔尔杰维奇王朝统治中断。

self-determination, the political process was not democratic: the government of Serbia concluded an agreement with elite Croatian groups, leaving the mass of the people dissatisfied with the new unitary state. The arrangement gave Serbia huge advantages, which enabled it to dominate the union and develop centralized rule. In 1919 the state was named Yugoslavia, and in April of the same year workers and other lower-class groups unhappy with the new situation formed the Socialist Party, which in 1920 was renamed the Communist Party of Yugoslavia. The great majority of Croatian parliamentary deputies favored a federal constitution and voted against

1 圣维特斯日，塞尔维亚传统的国庆和宗教盛会日，即每年的6月15日（罗马儒略历），这一天也是格里历（公历）的6月28日
2 建立
3 单一的；统一的
4 极权主义
5 暗杀；行刺
6 摄政；摄政统治

the 1920 Vidovdan[1] (St.Vitus's Day) Constitution, which abolished the traditional regions and instituted[2] centralized and unitary[3] rule by Serbia, but the Serbs won the vote and the federalist block was broken.

King Aleksandar and his Serb-dominated government were bitterly opposed by the Croatian Republican Peasant Party, led by Stjepan Radić, who was shot in 1928, inside the National Assembly. This represented the beginning of the royal dictatorship. Aleksandar abolished the constitution and parliament in January 1929, and banned all activities by political parties. In opposition to the King's totalitarianism[4], the middle classes in Croatia and Serbia formed the "united opposition". However, the main force and engine of democratic and opposition movements was the Communist Party of Yugoslavia (KPJ) led by Josip Broz Tito, who was elected to the post in 1937. Aleksandar was assassinated[5] in 1934, and as his son, Peter II, was a minor, a regency[6] council dominated by his cousin Prince Paul took over the role of king. In 1939, after long negotiations, the council was forced to accept an agreement between Prime Minister Dragisa Cvjetković and Vladko Maček, of the Croatian Peasant Party that ensured Croatia a form of autonomy.

The Second World War (1941–45)

At the beginning of the Second World War, when Hungary, Romania[1], Bulgaria[2], and Slovakia took Hitler's side, Yugoslavia faced a political and social crisis: the government led by Cvjetković and Maček supported Germany, but the people were strongly against it. The Communist Party started mass demonstrations, while army conspirators[3] in Serbia proclaimed Peter II king. Taking advantage of the confusion, Hitler easily occupied Yugoslavia after only eleven days, and the state fell apart: Slovenia was divided between Italy and Germany, the majority of Dalmatia (the Croatian coastline and islands) was occupied by the Italians, and the bulk of inland Croatia came under Hungarian rule. Hitler and Mussolini[4] installed Ante

1 罗马尼亚（欧洲巴尔干半岛东北部国家）
2 保加利亚（欧洲东南部国家）
3 阴谋者；同谋者
4 墨索里尼，意大利法西斯党首领及独裁者

乌斯塔沙运动 (Ustaše Movement)

1929 年由安特·帕维里奇和古斯塔夫·波切克等人成立；成立初期仅仅是一个搞恐怖活动的民族主义政治组织，后演变成克罗地亚的右翼组织，它统治下的"克罗地亚独立国"在 1941 年参加了轴心国集团，打上了深深的法西斯烙印，该运动组织于 1945 年被南斯拉夫人民军歼灭。

Pavelić, leader of the fascist **Ustaše movement**, as leader of the puppet[1] Independent State of Croatia[2] (NDH).

This was a hard time for liberal-minded people: the Ustaše regime created a reign of terror in which absolute obedience[3] was enforced, and nowadays most Croats utterly condemn the atrocities[4] of the NDH. Opposition to the NDH was led by the Communist Party. While the Communists were waging a partisan war, rival royalist "Chetnik[5]" forces were working to establish Greater Serbia, and their leader, Draža Mihajlović, refused to cooperate with the partisans[6]. He eventually collaborated with the Italians in order to oppose both the Ustaše and the partisans. This caused the Western Allies to

1 傀儡国
2 克罗地亚独立国（1941–1945），受乌斯塔沙运动组织统治，但实际上是德国纳粹扶持的傀儡政权，领土包含克罗地亚（不含达尔马提亚）和波斯尼亚和黑塞哥维那和斯洛文尼亚北部及塞尔维亚的伏伊伏丁那部分
3 顺从；服从
4 暴行；残忍
5 特指两次世界大战中南斯拉夫塞维尔游击战士
6 游击队员

withdraw their support, and in 1944 King Peter dismissed Mihajlović as Chief of Staff of the Yugoslav Army in the Fatherland and replaced him with **Tito**.

The Socialist Federal Republic of Yugoslavia (1945–90)

Croatia became one of six republics in Tito's Yugoslavia, also called the Second Yugoslavia, or the Socialist Federal Republic of Yugoslavia, established in 1945. This Communist government was very different from those prevailing in neighboring countries: private property was nationalized but living standards were much higher than in other Communist countries. Tito

铁托 (Tito, 1892–1980)

前南斯拉夫社会主义联邦共和国总统、南斯拉夫共产主义者联盟总书记、南斯拉夫人民军元帅；在二战中领导南斯拉夫人民进行反法西斯运动，做出重要的贡献；二战后坚持“南斯拉夫人的南斯拉夫”原则，与苏联关系破裂，危机重重，但铁托以强硬手段维护了南斯拉夫的统一。

1 分红制，利益分配
2 华沙条约，原名《友好合作互助条约》，简称华约。苏联、捷克斯洛伐克、保加利亚、匈牙利、民主德国、波兰、罗马尼亚、阿尔巴尼亚八国于 1955 年 5 月 14 日在波兰华沙签订。之后，华沙条约组织正式成立，成为与以美国为首的北大西洋公约组织对峙的政治、军事集团。1991 年 7 月，该条约失效
3 不结盟的；中立的
4 贝尔格莱德（塞尔维亚共和国首都）
5 再次点燃；重新激起…
6 镇压
7 反感；厌恶

established an effective system of profit-sharing[1] decentralized workers' councils, and there was arguably a greater degree of personal freedom and engagement with the West. Tito resisted pressure from Moscow to join the Warsaw Pact[2], and pursued a neutral foreign policy as a leader of the non-aligned[3] movement. However, Serbia was still the center of the federal state: money, military power, economic strength, and political influence were based in Belgrade[4].

Over time, tensions mounted, reigniting[5] the national spirit. In the 1970s, the Croatian Spring political movement campaigned for greater civil, cultural, and political rights. The leading cultural organization, Matica Hrvatska, declared the Croatian language to be separate from Serbian. In 1971, Zagreb University students went on strike calling for Communist Party reform. Tito responded with a crackdown[6]. Perhaps inevitably, after Tito's death in 1980, the antipathy[7] between the republics of Yugoslavia rose to the surface and led to its violent breakup. Political life became more active, partly because there was now no one with the charisma and influence to hold the nations together, and partly because the idea of national states grew stronger as people became more mature and self-aware. Meanwhile, Serbia, under Slobodan Milošević, was reverting to hardline[1] Communism.

The Parting of the Ways (1990)

Following the rejection of Slovenia's demands for independence of each of the national Communist parties, Slovenia and Croatia walked out of the Congress of the Yugoslav League of Communists in 1990. That year, free elections for the Croatian parliament and municipal assemblies were held, and the reformed Communists were defeated by the Croatian Democratic Union (HDZ), led by **Franjo Tudjman**, who became president.

[1] 强硬路线；强硬派

弗拉尼奥·图季曼 (Franjo ludjman, 1922–1999)

克罗地亚前总统，是 1991 年克罗地亚脱离南斯拉夫联盟独立战争的领袖。

Croatia quickly devised a constitution and became a representative parliamentary democracy.

The Croatian War of Independence (1991–95)

On June 25, 1991, the Croatian parliament passed a declaration of independence from Yugoslavia. That same year the Yugoslav army, directed by Serbian President Slobodan Milošević, started a war that ended in 1995 with the victory and recognition of Croatia. In 1992 Croatia become a member of the UN.

The Homeland War

The War of Independence, also known as the "**Homeland War**," started in the summer of 1991 when Serbs from Croatia's mountainous areas, where they constituted a relative majority, rebelled and formed an unrecognized "Autonomous Region of the Serb Krajina." Croats living in the region

克罗地亚战争 (Homeland War)

指的是 1990 年到 1995 年之间，克罗地亚从南斯拉夫独立出来时克罗地亚人和塞尔维亚人之间因民族对立引发的战争。

were expelled.

Attempts at intervention by the Croatian police were obstructed[1] by the federal Yugoslav army (YNA). The conflict culminated[2] with the socalled "log revolution," when the Serbs from Krajina blocked the roads to the tourist destinations in Dalmatia with logs. All remaining ties with Yugoslavia were cut in October 1991.

The border on east was at the city of Vukovar[3], which underwent a three-month siege and thus became a "hero town" for Croats and a symbol of national pride, although it eventually fell to Serbian forces on November 18, 1991. It is still hotly debated whether the city could have been saved if the West had acted decisively to stop the devastation and war crimes committed there.

1 阻塞；妨碍
2 （以某种结果）告终
3 武科瓦尔（克罗地亚东部边境城市）
4 侵略；进攻
5 国家地位

To dissuade the YNA from further aggression[4], the EU countries recognized Croatian statehood[5] in January 1992. Following UN-brokered ceasefires, the YNA forces retreated from Croatia into neighboring Bosnia-Herzegovina,

igniting war there, and as a consequence Croatia was flooded with more than 700,000 refuges from Bosnia, most of them Muslims.

In 1995, Croatia started **Operation Storm** and quickly reconquered most of the so-called Republic of Serbian Krajina[1]. A few months later the war was ended by negotiations leading to the Dayton Agreement[2] in November 1995, the General Framework Agreement for Peace in Bosnia and Herzegovina.

On November 6, 1996, Croatia became a member of the Council of Europe. Peaceful integration of the remaining Serbian-controlled territories in eastern Slavonia was completed in 1998 under UN supervision.

Modern Croatia

After the death of Franjo Tudjman, the first president of the Republic of Croatia, in late

1 塞尔维亚克拉伊纳共和国（原克罗地亚克拉伊纳自治区，1991 年宣布独立后控制了克罗地亚与波黑边境的塞族地区）

2 代顿协议，1995 年 11 月由波斯尼亚和黑塞哥维那内战中交战的各方在美国俄亥俄州代顿市的莱特－特派森空军基地所签订的协议，同意中止这场长达三年八个月的血腥内战

风暴行动 (Operation Storm)

1995 年，克罗地亚军队发起“风暴行动”，仅用 36 小时便控制了公路并收复了西斯拉沃尼亚塞族区。

1999, new elections were held. Stjepan Mesić became the new president, and Ivica Racan prime minister, of a center-left[1] coalition. In November 2000, Croatia became a member of the World Trade Organization and less than a year after that, in October 2001, signed an association agreement with the European Union. Application for membership was formally submitted in February/March 2003.

In late 2003, Croatia elected a new prime minister, Ivo Sanader, and in 2004 the European Commission issued a recommendation that accession negotiations with Croatia should begin. The country received EU applicant status in June 2004, and negotiations started in May 2005. According to the expectations of both the Croatian government and the European Union, Croatia should become a member in 2009/10.

GOVERNMENT

Croatia is a democratic republic. From 1990 to 2000 it had a semi-presidential system; the new Račan government amended the constitution, and

1 左翼的

1 立法的；有立法权的
2 司法部；法官；司法制度

since 2000 it has had a parliamentary system.

The president is the head of state, elected by popular vote for a five-year term. The same president may not serve more than two terms. He has limited executive powers but is in charge of the armed forces and represents the country at home and abroad.

Parliament (the *Sabor*), which has legislative[1] power, consists of 100 to 160 members who are elected by popular vote to serve a four-year term.

The prime minister is the head of government (*Vlada*), which keeps executive power. Government ministers (fourteen in total, each in charge of a particular portfolio) are appointed by the president with the consent of parliament. The judiciary[2] is independent and has three tiers: the Supreme Court, county courts, and municipal courts, while there is also a Constitutional Court ruling on matters regarding the constitution.

Politics

The Croatian Communist Party (SKH) was the only party permitted in socialist Yugoslavia between 1945 and 1990. But from 1990, when the first multiparty elections took place, until today, the political scene has become much richer. The left-wing parties have generally moderated their economic stance in the last ten years, resulting in a political center enlarged with center-left and center-right parties and coalitions. The further south you go, the greater the influence of right-wing parties. In Istria, there is a strong local party with almost no competition, and in the east, right-wing nationalist parties are in the ascendant[1].

Politics is a powerful tool in the business life of the country, because civil institutions are still in a phase of development and NGOs[2] are growing in number and influence, so having politically sympathetic people in the right places can speed the way to success.

Some of the most prominent parties are the Croatian Democratic Union (HDZ—right-wing

1 优势；支配地位
2 国际非政府组织

conservative Christian Democrats), the Social Democratic Party of Croatia (SDP—left-wing successor of the Communist Party of Croatia), the Croatian Social Liberal Party (HSLS—the left center party founded in 1989, in Communist times), the Croatian Party of Rights (HSP—right wing), the Croatian Peasants' Party (HSS—right center), and the Croatian People's Party (HNS—liberal democrats of the center). Most campaigning is done on television, which is by far the most influential political medium.

THE ECONOMY

Croatia has had to deal with postwar economic problems as well as the aftereffects of Communist politics. The privatization of national property in the Tudjman era was both highly suspect and effected with many failures, increasing the number of unemployed to 22.3 percent in 2002 and ruining some companies through poor business planning and strategy.

During the last five years, GDP growth has averaged 4.7 percent, which means that GDP in 2006 in comparison to 2000 was up 25.7 percent. The increase has been most significant in manufacturing, trade, tourism, construction, and transportation services, which together represent the most important branches of the Croatian economy.

Inflation in Croatia is low (about 2 percent) and economic growth is estimated at 4.5–5 percent per annum. GDP in 2005 was 7,000 euros per capita, while according to the statistics for 2006, GDP will increase to 4.8 percent. According to the report on global competitiveness for 2007, Croatia took fifty-seventh place (Turkey is in fifty-ninth place, Slovenia in thirty-seventh). The fastest-growing sectors are real estate and finance.

Today unemployment is around 12 percent, the lowest since 1995. In general Croats are not fond of moving to find work. In some cities the unemployment rate is high, while in others companies are advertising for staff. Differing attitudes reflect the years of Communist life: the older generation is not used to thinking in terms

of a free market and competition, expecting to have a job for life, while the young are very much aware of the realities of the new capitalist environment.

The Croatian economy is currently in a period of transition, adjusting its procedures to conform to EU legislation.

Chapter 02

VALUES & ATTITUDES

The Croats are hedonists[1]. They are outgoing, expressive[2], and noisy. Meanness and coldness are disliked; what they appreciate are big appetites and spontaneous behavior. They are, however, very proud of their country and sensitive about national issues. There are consequently some values they hold particularly dear, and some important taboos[3] to remember when dealing with them. It is said that there are three things sacred to Croats: the flag, the Virgin Mary[4], and football. The first two will be covered in this chapter, the last in Chapter 5, Daily Life.

The differences between the younger generation (up to the early forties) and the older

1 享乐主义者
2 富于表情的，有表现力的
3 （文化或宗教习俗方面的）禁忌，忌讳，戒律
4 《圣经》中耶稣的母亲。据福音书记载，她是童贞女，由“圣灵感孕”而生耶稣。天主教、东正教尊之为“童贞圣母”

1 不可调和的，不能协调的
2 部落的，种族的
3 重视商业的
4 破坏性的，具有颠覆性的
5 天主教（基督教三大派系之一）

generation are great: their value systems are different and sometimes irreconcilable[1]. The wise foreigner will take account of which age group he or she is dealing with and adapt his or her approach accordingly. Older Croats grew up under a political system that promised lifetime security. Husbands were in charge, and were respected by all the members of the family in a sort of tribal[2] structure with strong family ties. In contrast, the young are more business-oriented[3], independent, ready for change, and open to new things, even if new means strange or subversive[4]. The family is still important to them, but ties are more relaxed and less formal. One of the main things that visitors should bear in mind is that Croatia was part of the Communist bloc but is now independent, with a strongly Catholic[5] sense of identity.

NATIONAL PRIDE AND IDENTITY

Croats are extremely proud of their nationality. For the visitor, the main points to remember are that the Croats should not be lumped in with other nations from ex-Yugoslavia, and that they did not start the war in the 1990s but defended themselves against Serb aggression. The value of being aware of these basic points should not be underestimated. The *leitmotif*[1] of Croatian identity surviving waves of foreign rulers can be found in the works of the Croatian writer **Miroslav Krleža**, a shaper of national consciousness and an icon[2] of Croatian literature whose work has been translated into English. Like **James Joyce** in *A Portrait of the Artist as a Young Man*, Krleža sought "to forge in the smithy[3] of his soul the uncreated conscience of his race". That same premium on[4] maintaining Croatian identity can lead to Eurosceptic[5] attitudes in a certain percentage of the population.

1 （音乐）主旋律；主旨，主题
2 偶像
3 铁匠铺，锻冶场
4 重视，珍视
5 欧洲怀疑论者，反对欧洲一体化者

克尔莱扎 (Miroslav Krleža, 1893–1981)

克罗地亚小说家，剧作家，出身于萨格勒布市一资产阶级家庭，代表作有《加利齐亚》《果尔果达》《狼谷》以及《格列姆巴伊老爷们》《垂死挣扎》《丽达》三部曲和《阿雷特伊》等。

詹姆斯·乔伊斯 (James Joyce, 1882–1941)

爱尔兰作家、诗人，二十世纪最伟大的作家之一，后现代文学的奠基者之一。其代表作有短篇小说集《都柏林人》，长篇小说《尤利西斯》和《芬尼根的守灵夜》等，其作品及"意识流"思想对世界文坛影响巨大。

Croats express their pride by cheering wildly for their home team at football matches, by waving flags at wedding parades, by singing patriotic[1] songs, and by being touchy[2] when lumped together with Serbs, Bosnians, Slovenians, or the Balkans in general. While educated people are not usually offended by this last classification—they know that Croatia is partly in the Balkans—you should still be careful not to raise political issues unless you are sure that you are in the right company. You'll notice that even over coffee questions of politics, provincial attitudes, and small-mindedness[3] come out of nowhere. Frustrating though it may be, it is best not to engage in such conversations and to stay silent if possible. Should you be asked to take sides, unless

1 爱国的
2 易生气的，难以取悦的
3 心胸狭窄，固执己见，气量小

you are well acquainted with the subject and have strong arguments, try to use the opportunity to encourage the protagonists[1] in the debate to explain the issues to you and describe what they have personally experienced. This can be a good way of getting a firsthand[2] overview, as well as winning some Brownie points[3] with your hosts.

Very much linked to national pride is the feeling of belonging[4] to the Catholic Church. In some communities (particularly smaller towns and villages or islands), being a good Croat is almost synonymous[5] with being a good Catholic. The Church is seen as the savior[6] of Croatian identity during Yugoslavia era and a keeper of national traditions and values.

ATTITUDES TOWARD FOREIGNERS

The older generation is generally conservative[7]. As they have not lived in a culture of traveling, they might be surprised to see a black person in Croatia, but are unlikely to harbor[8] truly xenophobic[9] feelings. In fact, the smaller the community, the warmer the welcome is likely to be—if the

1 主人公；主要人物，领导者
2 第一手的
3 印象分（原意指美国 7 至 10 岁女童子军因成绩或善行而得的积分）
4 归属
5 与……同名的
6 救世主
7 保守的
8 怀有，心怀（尤指反面感情或想法）
9 恐惧外国人的

[1] 盗用，侵吞
[2] 流行的，普遍的；广传的
[3] 斯堪的纳维亚半岛的

visitor demonstrates a sympathetic approach. As long as a visitor shows Croatians respect in the ways indicated above he or she should have no problems. Croats do not expect foreigners to speak their language but greatly appreciate it if they use a few basic words and phrases, such as *Dobar dan* (Good day), *Hvala* (Thank you), or *Kako ste?* (How are you?).

Owing to the way the free market was introduced, and the bad economic situation that forced many people to sell their properties to foreigners after the Homeland War, you might come across the view that foreigners are people who come to buy or appropriate[1] Croatian land and natural resources for their business or pleasure. This is not a widely prevalent[2] attitude, but can be found on the islands in particular.

Due primarily to the support given during the Homeland War, Croats tend to be more open toward Germans (and people from Scandinavian[3] countries, to where many Croats fled) than to the British or French. The manner in which a foreigner approaches them is very important: an ignorant or superior attitude—and, rightly or wrongly, the British have a reputation for this in Croatia—will not win any sympathy. In general terms, it is as well to remember that the Balkan Peninsula is among the bloodiest battlefields[1] in Europe, and that all its peoples carry a heavy burden of history on their shoulders.

Regarding minorities, Serbs are the largest (see below). Other minorities, such as Italians, Austrians, Czechs[2], or Gypsies[3], are very low in number, and there is no special sensitivity[4] in relation to them. The Czechs are a very active minority, holding traditional festivals in Slavonia, as the Italian minority do in Istria, where they also have an Italian school, making it easier for young people to apply to Italian universities. The Chinese are a new addition to the scene: most live by trading, opening small shops with cheap and low-quality goods. Gypsies can be seen in the poorer districts of big towns, living by begging or playing music on the streets. In the suburbs and small rural communities they

1 战场
2 捷克人
3 吉普赛人
4 敏感性，敏感度

attend state schools.

ATTITUDES TOWARD SERBS

On the sensitive question of the Serbs, as with a few other issues, the Croats are divided between those who think that the past is the past and should be left there, and those who still feel bitter and look back in anger. The first group votes for normalizing[1] the relationship and establishing trading relations, seeing their eastern neighbor as one of their best markets, which is certainly true, while the other group would rather keep east in the east and as far as possible from Croatia. The wounds from the Homeland War are still fresh—Croatia is till trying to trace around two thousand missing people who got "lost" in Serbian prisons and were probably executed in secret—and the ongoing[2] legal processes at the Hague[3] are far from over. Happily, the prevailing attitude is the first one—Serbs continue to come to the Croatian coastline, business is done, and trade is growing. The same is true for Montenegro and Bosnia.

1 使正常化，使正规化
2 不间断的，正在进行的
3 海牙（荷兰西部城市，联合国国际法院所在地）

APPEARANCE MATTERS

Although there is not yet a widespread culture of foreign travel, the culture of dress is flourishing, at times even bordering on ostentation[1]. Looking good is more important for women than for men, but both pay a great deal of attention to appearance, designer clothes, fashion, and style. Health and fitness[2] centers and other beauty treatments are "in" in Croatia.

Everyone who comes to Croatia will notice that locals spend considerable sums of money on clothes and cars. As a nation they are goodlooking people: tall and toned, and mostly darkhaired. The men are well built and broadshouldered. Croats like wearing Italian and French designer clothes, and favor refined and sophisticated styles over cutting-edge[3] fashion.

HUMOR AND SEX

Humor is an important part of life, and may still be used as a way of coping with the bad experiences of the past. Croats joke about two main subjects—sex and politics—but sex is the

1 卖弄；招摇
2 健康
3 前沿的

favorite topic at any point and on any occasion. Even at business meetings it is not uncommon for jokes to go around the conference table.

Croats like traditional humor, which combines slapstick[1], wordplay[2], and situation comedy—*Monty Python*[3], for instance, was very popular. Don't be surprised by their openness and ease with sexual allusions[4], and their use of "dirty" words, including swearing. They love jokes about Mujo and Haso, two imaginary stereotypical Bosnians, still popular from Yugoslavian times, and their woman, Fata.

SAM SVOJ MAJSTOR—DO-IT-YOURSELF

The Croats are inclined to think they can do everything that needs to be done by themselves: the heating, the painting, the building, the decorating. So mechanics and skilled craftsmen[5] are rarely needed: there is always at least a friend who can help with all the house jobs or car repairs. You'll get used to being thought strange when you call a plumber[6] to fix your broken washing machine instead of doing it yourself — but you

1 打闹剧，粗俗滑稽剧
2 双关语，俏皮话
3 巨蟒剧团，1965 年 10 月 5 日第一次出现在观众的视野中，由五位英国人和一位美国人组成。他们的电视喜剧作品《飞翔的马戏团》经由 BBC 播出后，很快成为了英国现代文化的一个标志。也正是从《飞翔的马戏团》开始，“巨蟒”逐渐为世界所熟知，并以自己独特的幽默方式开创了一种被全世界（尤其是好莱坞）广泛效仿和套用的喜剧类型
4 暗示
5 工匠，手艺人
6 水管工

should expect to pay good money for it.

MEN AND WOMEN

Croatian society is traditional in that the man is officially the head of the household, but one of the most popular proverbs[1] says "The woman holds three corners of the house, the man just one." This shows the importance of women and the key role of the family in Croatian society—but it also just as clearly indicates where a woman belongs.

With the new generation this has changed as well: men are now sharing in housework and childcare. Paternity leave[2] is approved for men, while woman can serve in the army equally with men, and can even be pilots.

The turning point in the male–female relationship came a few years ago. There is no doubt that domestic violence was always there, but according to statistics, women started to report their husbands and partners who were beating them and their children. NGOs are very active today in protecting women's and children's rights, opening safe houses, and providing legal

1 谚语，格言
2 （父亲）陪产假

advice services and lawyers for court cases free of charge.

In Croatian society it is appreciated if a woman is a good cook and nourishes her "feminine[1]" virtues—kindness, modesty, and gentleness. In this country, men like to be "real" men and have what they consider to be real women by their side. They also think it is their primary role to support the family and earn money. But when it comes to education, women predominate[2] among the ranks of the highly educated. They tend to finish their studies before men, and in total have more academic degrees than men; but for the same job, they are still paid less than their male colleagues.

Homosexuality[3] is still widely considered disgusting, and public displays of intimacy[4] by gay people are not recommended. Having said that, gay rights campaigners[5] are active in Croatia, and in 2007 they were allowed for the first time to put their flags on the main square in Zagreb and publicly advertise their parade.

1 女性的
2 占主导（或支配）地位；占优势
3 同性恋
4 亲昵行为，亲密关系
5 活动家

THE FAMILY

The family has an important role, as do lifelong friendships. It is common for couples to live together before marriage, but after a while they exchange vows and raise children within marriage. Children born out of wedlock[1] are viewed with a certain distaste[2].

Family festivities, such as name days and Church holidays, are obligatory[3]. On those occasions godparents[4], who are regarded as family members, join in the celebrations, and such rituals are repeated year after year, strengthening family ties as time goes by.

Everyday conversation at work includes chitchat[5] about family matters, children, home meals, and family weekends. Keeping photographs of your children or perhaps your partner in your wallet is common. Croats will gladly speak about their family, and this is a good way to start a conversation or break an uncomfortable silence.

In business, family and family ties play a significant role: family firms are common, and are typically found in professions such as medicine,

1 婚姻
2 厌恶，讨厌
3 必须的，强制性的
4 教父和教母，天主教、正教以及有些新教宗教行洗礼时为受洗者设置的保证人和监护人
5 聊天，闲谈

1 牙医业
2 饮食业
3 布道，训诫
4 交织，穿插
5 垄断
6 大众
7 动机
8 社交，交际
9 声明，主张，要求

dentistry[1], law, and catering[2].

RELIGION

Statistics show that more than 95 percent of Croats are Roman Catholic, and as we have seen the Catholic Church is closely associated with national identity. Although Church and state are constitutionally separate, sermons[3] are very often interwoven[4] with politics, and politicians are always prominent at any Church holiday or religious celebration. It is true to say that the Catholic Church preserved Croatian traditions during Yugoslavia times, when believers had to hide their faith, but it is equally true to admit that today the Church has a monopoly[5] of political influence and strong control over the opinions of the masses[6]. Croats are quite regular once-a-week churchgoers, but their motivation[7] is not purely religious—being seen at church is important. Church is also a place for socializing[8]—coffee bars around churches are full on Sundays. Visiting a church on a Catholic holiday is obligatory: it is an assertion[9] of national identity more than religion.

In line with that, children in state elementary schools have (Catholic) scripture[1] classes as part of the school curriculum. Though they are said not to be compulsory[2], any child not attending is considered strange and is asked for an explanation.

With regard to abortion, Croatia officially allows terminations[3] in hospitals until the twelfth week of pregnancy, but the Church continuously crusades[4] against this legal right, demanding that parliament outlaw[5] abortion and punish the practice. Another question that concerns the Church is that of working on Sundays.

Other religions, Christian and non-Christian, can be found in Croatia, and are freely practiced; but generally speaking Croats are traditionalists, and Protestants[6], along with Buddhists[7] or Muslims[8], are silently regarded as "different." Croats are not strongly against other religions, and show tolerance, but most of them would not be happy to see their child marrying someone belonging to any other faith than Catholic. The philosophy of Buddhism is quite popular among the young, who find the dogma[9] and the rules of

1 圣经
2 必修的
3 结束，终止
4 长期坚定不移的奋斗
5 宣布……为不合法的
6 新教徒（新教即基督教新教，是由16世纪宗教改革运动中脱离罗马天主教会的教会和教徒形成的一系列新宗派的统称。与“天主教”“正教”并称基督教三大派别）
7 佛教徒
8 穆斯林教徒
9 教条，教理

[1] 限制性的，约束的
[2] 剧变，动荡

Catholicism old-fashioned and restrictive[1]. Yoga, nutrition, and meditation are the most respected aspects of Buddhist teaching.

STATUS, POWER, AND MONEY

Until the 1990s, there was little inequality in Croatian society. Most people had apartments, cars, education, steady jobs, summerhouses, and pensions. With the political upheavals[2] of that decade, this has changed as well, and a classless society has become an aspirational, classobsessed society. No Scandinavian-style modesty for the Croatians: they like to show off a new car or boat, build a house, and buy property at the seaside. According to statistics, some of the most expensive hotels in Croatia take their greatest numbers of bookings from Croats, not from rich foreigners, as might be assumed. Croats love to spend money in restaurants and shops, even when they do not have it. Living beyond one's means is common here: almost everyone is in the red, but skiing trips, summer vacations, and a new car are a must for many. Everyone uses credit cards for nearly everything.

In Croatian society today success is generally measured by money. Although the Church and civil institutions warn against the dangers of such an attitude, it is still the prevailing view of a society in which the value of knowledge is trumped[1] by the power of money. The situation is more complicated when you take a look at the legal system: justice is slow and people generally do not have faith in it. Therefore knowing the right people is the key to success and having influential friends is one of the most desirable social values.

Education is becoming more and more important, but still only 8 percent of people go on to higher education, and compulsory education ends with elementary school. It is understandable if what we've said above is taken into account—money counts for more than knowledge. For that very reason many educated Croats leave for the USA or Western European countries, where they stay for the rest of their lives.

[1] 胜过，打败

1 遗留的感觉，沿袭下来的风俗（或思想等）
2 心态
3 （两件事之间的）间歇

WORK ETHIC

It is also worth saying something about the Croatian work ethic. Partly as a hangover[1] from Yugoslavia times, when everyone had a steady job with a guaranteed salary, and when overtime did not exist, and partly as a consequence of their mentality[2] and life values, Croats put in their hours fairly, but then they want to go home and have some time to themselves. Friendship is, as we have seen, more important than work, and since overtime is rarely rewarded by extra payment, many employees, particularly the older ones, are not eager to stay on beyond the obligatory eight hours. Most companies have flexible working hours. The day begins between 8:00 and 9:00 a.m., but breaks are not strictly fixed and coffee interludes[3] happen several times a day.

There are big differences between the private and public sectors and between the younger and older generations, but the prevailing view that diligence and long hours will not make you rich and successful influences attitudes to work. For that reason most Croatians prefer to work for international corporations[1] where salaries are bigger and the opportunities to get ahead are given to those with knowledge or expertise[2]. In short, Croatians are good workers when they are treated fairly and paid well for what they do.

About 18 percent of the population live below the poverty line, which is comparable to the UK, for example, but the buying power of the British poor is twice that of the Croatian poor. By contrast, the rich in Croatia are very rich indeed, and tend to hedonism and conspicuous[3] consumption. On the other hand, no matter how large your income is, it would be regarded as shameful and impolite to split a dinner bill: one person pays for everything, but there is an unwritten rule that if you have been treated to dinner, you should return the favor with an invitation for another dinner within a month or two at most and, of course, foot the bill.

1 公司
2 专门知识；专门技术
3 显著的，显而易见的

Chapter

03

FESTIVALS & TRADITIONS

[1] 名义上地；有名无实地

Although Croatia is more than 87 percent Catholic, with the strong influence of the Church evident in politics and social attitudes, most holidays, whether public or religious, are observed only nominally[1] by the large majority of people and are seen primarily as a time to rest. This means that even Croats themselves may not know which events particular festivals celebrate, but recognize the holidays as red-letter days in the calendar meaning time off from work.

The big festivals, such as Christmas and Easter, have well-established rituals and traditions, while celebrations of weddings, birthdays, and name days vary from family to family and depend very much on whether the person feted[1] is part of a rural or urban community.

Beside public holidays, when everyone is off work, local celebrations that are not included in this national calendar, such as the local patron saint's day[2] or special fishermen's celebrations, are important and respected. Information about these can be obtained at any local tourist office. Also, most businesses, fruit and vegetable markets, shops, and shopping centers will, with a very few exceptions, be closed on public holidays. There will be far fewer people about town, and policemen

PUBLIC HOLIDAYS	
January 1	New Year's Day
January 6	Epiphany
March/April	Easter Monday
May 1	Labor Day
June 7	Corpus Christi
June 22	Anti-Fascist Resistance Day
June 25	Croatian National Day
August 5	Victory Day and National Thanksgiving Day
October 8	Independence Day
November 1	All Saints' Day
December 25–26	Christmas

1 宴请；招待
2 守护神节

will wear parade uniforms, but apart from that there will be few clues to what is being celebrated. There is one sure indication of whether it is a public or religious occasion: if there are flags on the houses, it's a public holiday.

It is common to make a "bridge" and connect holidays with weekends. Some companies even agree to formalize such a bridge on a corporate level by officially allocating one or two days from the annual holiday entitlement of their employees to dates falling between holidays and weekends.

CHRISTMAS

While Christmas itself begins on Christmas Eve, December 24, when families go to Midnight Mass[1], the start of the Christmas season is December 5, the eve of St. Nicholas's Day. At this time an old man in white with a long white beard can be seen on the streets with a bag on his shoulders. Behind him goes Krampus[2], the humpbacked[3] devil, in red and black. People on the streets and town squares sell gold-sprayed[4] birches[5] reserved for badly behaved children, and also as a warning to the

1 子夜弥撒，通常午夜在教堂内举行，以表示圣诞日的开始
2 克拉普斯，北欧圣诞神话人物，相传是圣尼古拉斯的随从，长得很吓人，头上长着两只角，全身长毛，看起来像恶鬼，专门惩罚坏小孩
3 驼背的
4 喷金的
5 桦树；桦木

well-behaved ones that they should stay as they are and keep away from ugly, horned Krampus. There are usually bright and cheerful open-air Christmas fairs on the streets, with stands full of colorful gifts for the coming celebrations.

People work on December 24, but generally just until midday, or 3:00 p.m. at the latest. Members of the close family join together on Christmas Eve, and the Christmas tree is decorated by the children that evening: people like to have a real tree and usually buy them potted. Gifts are placed under the tree and should not be opened before midnight. Since Croatian independence the biblical[1] story of the baby Jesus can be publicly told. His arrival—and that of the presents—is announced by one of the grown-up family members ringing a small bell while the children are in the other room. (During Yugoslavia times a tree was decorated on New Year's Eve, and New Year presents were supposedly brought by Santa Claus[2].)

The Christmas Eve meal is modest, and avoids sugar, fat, and meat. Fish and vegetables

1 圣经的；依据圣经的

2 圣诞老人，西方圣诞神话人物，又称圣·尼古拉斯；相传于每年的圣诞前夕会驾乘由9只驯鹿拉的雪橇，挨家挨户地从烟囱进入屋里，给好孩子送礼物；圣诞老人一般头戴红色圣诞帽子，大大的白色胡子，一身红色棉衣，脚穿红色靴子

are traditional. The most commonly served dish is salted cod, which is prepared in different ways—as pâté[1], in a stew, or with potatoes—but is always spicy and aromatic[2].

Friends are usually invited for lunch the next day, December 25, when a meat dish called *sarma* is obligatory on the menu. *Sarma* is a combination of spicy minced meat with rice wrapped in pickled[3] cabbage leaves and cooked for hours in a large pot on a small fire with pieces of smoked meat and a spicy sauce. On this day meat, sugar, and fat can be used as much as wanted. Older women, and women in traditional families, will bake bite-sized cakes and cookies for weeks before Christmas—in the old days it was a minor scandal if at least a dozen varieties were not made, including walnut[4] loaf and poppy-seed[5] rolls with raisins. Today women do not bake so much, but serving bought varieties is not popular.

Some weeks before Christmas people sow wheat grains in a pot, which they put on the table as a symbol of good luck for the coming year. In traditional families and in rural communities, there

1 头盘
2 芳香的，芬芳的
3 腌制的；盐渍的
4 胡桃；核桃
5 罂粟籽

is an old custom of bringing straw into the house and putting it under the table. This symbolizes Jesus' birth in a stable, and is also a reminder of the modesty that should be maintained during this season—although Christmas is actually becoming more and more commercialized.

NEW YEAR

In recent years it has become popular to welcome in the New Year on the streets with lots of people and fireworks. In the past, people would go to restaurants and hotels or celebrate at home. More gifts are exchanged, placed under the tree on New Year's Eve for the children to find on New Year's Day. Since Christmas is generally more important and given greater value, New Year gifts are only small and symbolic. The traditional New Year lunch menu consists of *sarma* and roast pork. There is a reason for the choice of pork: since the pig turns the ground over with its snout[1], eating it is a symbol of progress in the New Year. Bigger companies organize a present-giving ceremony for employees' children, or add a "child supplement" to salaries.

1 口鼻部

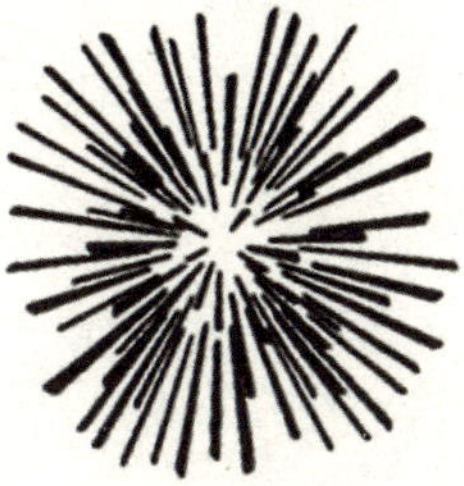

1 复活
2 自制；放弃；避免

EASTER

Easter is the most important Christian holiday. It is called *Uskrs* ("Resurrection[1]"), and preparations are undertaken by the devout throughout the week before, Holy Week. Believers will abstain[2] from something they like, such as eating sweets or meat, or drinking wine, in order to enter Easter in an enhanced state of purity.

On the first day of Holy Week people go to church with olive branches blessed by priests. It is believed they bring peace and prosperity to private and business life. The peak of Easter time starts on Holy Thursday (in Croatia "Great Thursday"): church bells are tied up for the next three days and farmers stay away from their fields. Good Friday is the only day in the year when Holy Mass is not celebrated. All these days, including Easter Monday, are dedicated to the family, and no public celebrations are

practiced.

One of the traditional customs is egg painting. Women used to dye the eggs by boiling them with onion peel or spinach[1], with the more creative and skillful spirits among them decorating them with wax, a practice known as "wax writing" though it was actually wax drawing (of flowers, ornaments, and abstract designs). Consequently Easter eggs in the continental part of Croatia are called *pisanice*, meaning "written ones". Today this custom is rarely seen in the towns, where people buy artificial colors and stickers.

A popular Easter game for children is egg knocking. Each child has an egg and tries to break the shell of the egg held by their partner. The one whose egg is broken has to surrender it to the winner, and the overall winner is, of course, the one with the largest collection of eggs.

On Easter Sunday people go to church carrying baskets of food: eggs, spring onions, cheese, cream, ham, and red radishes[2] are usual. The priest blesses the food, which is later consumed at home with close family. On Easter

1 菠菜
2 萝卜

[1] 康乃馨

Sunday people stay at home all day and the streets are empty. Easter Monday, however, is a day for visiting relatives or good friends for lunch.

LABOR DAY

Labor Day has become the first occasion of the year for a mass migration from towns and cities for a short vacation. Everyone who has somewhere or someone else to go to, or who can afford a hotel or a boat, takes a break from work and leaves for the coast or the hills to enjoy a few sunny days there. In Yugoslavia times this was a far more important holiday: women would be given a red carnation[1], and companies would organize celebrations for their employees. Today, among young people, it is a sort of joke (but not an offensive one) to give red flowers, or bring cookies to the office in honor of Labor Day.

Even so, public celebrations are still held and taken seriously: each town organizes an entertainment program in the park or at some convenient public venue, with traditional bean stew (so-called "military beans" cooked with meat in large pots on a small fire) served free to all. This day is also traditionally used by politicians and trade unionists[1] to raise important social matters such as workers' rights, working conditions, salaries, pensions, and similar topics.

CROATIAN NATIONAL DAY

Taking place on June 25 every year, this holiday celebrates the day in 1991 when the Croatian parliament (the *Sabor*) made the momentous[2] constitutional decision to vote for the independence and sovereignty[3] of the Republic of Croatia. This holiday is one of the three most important public holidays, the two others being Independence Day and Victory Day.

INDEPENDENCE DAY

Commemorating[4] October 8, 1991, when parliament approved the declaration cutting off all formal ties with the other republics of ex-Yugoslavia, this date is celebrated in Croatia as a public holiday and nonworking day.

1 工会会员
2 重要的；重大的
3 主权；主权国家
4 庆祝，纪念

[1] 烈士；殉道者

VICTORY DAY AND NATIONAL THANKSGIVING DAY

Victory Day and National Thanksgiving Day celebrate August 5, 1995, when the Croatian army liberated the town of Knin from the Yugoslav (Serb) army in the military operation called Storm. This was, and still is, a very emotional day for people, and symbolizes the strength of the Croatian nation and their determination to unite the entire territory of their republic.

ALL SAINTS' DAY

As a predominantly Catholic country, Croatia celebrates All Saints' Day in memory of the martyrs[1] of the church and of departed loved ones. People visit graveyards, bringing flowers and candles. There are special regulations governing public transportation and cars are not permitted.

PERSONAL HOLIDAYS

Summer Vacations

Croatians use most of their annual vacation

entitlement from mid-June to mid-September. As many people either have relatives who live at the seaside or have their own summerhouses on the coast or on one of the islands, renting apartments with full kitchens is not common. On the other hand, the well-off like to take villas or go to expensive hotels, so, contrary to what might be expected, foreigners are not necessarily the main guests of upscale residences. This again illustrates the Croatians' readiness to spend lavishly[1] on their pleasures.

The summer vacation can last from two to a maximum of five weeks, depending on working place, position, and sector. Also, for each child one gets an extra day.

Winter Vacations

Besides their summer vacation and spring break around Labor Day, Croats like to go skiing in winter. At this point you notice how well-off people are: those with plenty of money go to France and Switzerland; those with less go to Austria and Italy. The cheapest resorts are in Slovenia and Bosnia.

1 丰富地；浪费地

[1] 喇叭；号
[2] 按汽车喇叭，发出响号

Children also have a one-month winter vacation, which starts before Christmas and matches the skiing season in January.

FAMILY OCCASIONS

Weddings

Generally, wedding parties can be divided into two categories: big, mass events, and quieter, intimate gatherings. A couple can decide between a civil and a church ceremony or have both, but if you are married in church you do not need a separate civil ceremony, as is the case in some countries. The favorite place for civil ceremonies is Old City Hall in Zagreb, and the waiting list for a booking can be long. Weddings on working days are cheaper than on weekends.

Saturday is the favorite day for weddings, and on that day you will hear car horns[1] honking[2], to announce that a couple has just been married. Cars may be decorated with flowers and ribbons, and flags held out of the windows, high in the air.

Church marriage is common, but mainly because it is traditional. The Croatians follow their customs carefully and rarely skimp[1] on a wedding feast, even if the family is not rich. In the countryside, most of the village population may attend. In towns, weddings are a chance for all the distant relatives to come together for a reunion. It is not unusual, therefore, to have three hundred people at a wedding reception and to spend a huge amount of money on the occasion, with live music, vast quantities of food and drink, a huge choice of cakes, and of course, gifts in the form of presents or money for the young couple. The fathers of both the bride and the groom seem almost to compete with each other in showing off.

Typical wedding gifts are pieces of furniture, electronic and technical equipment, or contributions to the honeymoon. The best man is expected to give the best present (which means the most expensive one). Some couples make a list of items they need for their new life together, and guests agree upon who will buy what.

1 节省；克扣

Birthdays and Name Days

Older Croatians pay more attention to name days[1] than birthdays: in the Catholic calendar each day is dedicated to a saint, and the person whose name day it is prepares a meal—usually dinner— for the family. It is common to bring a small gift (wines are a good gift for a man, on any occasion) and flowers.

The younger generation gives priority to birthdays. At work, the person whose birthday it is brings cakes or cold meats for colleagues, who will have clubbed together to buy a small gift. Close friends are invited for dinner at home or at a restaurant, and everyone brings a gift. The person whose birthday it is pays the whole bill.

1 命名日是一项自中世纪流传下来的传统，该节日是和本人同名的圣徒纪念日，主要在一些天主教和东正教国家庆祝，但各国有自己的命名日体系

Chapter 04

MAKING FRIENDS

The main institution in Croatian society is the family. People socialize within a fixed circle of relations and school or college friends, and tend to have lifelong friendships. Friends are equal to members of the family, and ties are close and tight. In Croatian culture it is impolite to keep in touch with just a monthly phone call: friendships are important, and they must be nourished.

However, Croats are used to foreigners, not only because of tourism being the main industry, but also due to their history. A long list of foreign rulers was mentioned in Chapter 1. Another reason for this lack of xenophobia is the fact that Croatian intellectuals have historically traveled

¹ 公开的，坦率的

abroad to study in Italy, France, the Czech Republic, or Austria, and if you dig a bit below the surface you'll discover how many Croats have roots or relatives in those countries.

Even if you are in Croatia for only a few days' vacation, you will have the opportunity to meet Croatian people and get to know them a little, and if you are working in the country or have one Croatian friend it is quite easy to make some superficial contacts. But forming a real friendship is a more delicate matter, which takes some time, because, while the Croats are openhearted, they are not as "up-front[1]" as, say, North Americans.

FORMS OF ADDRESS

Croatians treat each other with respect. They have two different words for "you." *Ti* is the informal "you," and *vi* is the formal version. It is always a matter of agreement between two people whether they will communicate using *ti* or *vi*: when they meet and introduce themselves, they address each other formally, and continue to do so until the senior person suggests adopting the informal form of address. The suggestion does not come from the junior person.

While it is common to address senior managers formally, middle managers are likely to suggest the informal usage. However, it is not impolite to say that you would rather keep it formal. One more thing needs to be explained in connection with the formal address, *vi*: this form is normally written with small letters, but if the first letter is capitalized (*V*), it denotes even greater respect toward a person than if you address them in lowercase[1] only. Also, when someone introduces themselves, take note of whether they say their given name only, their surname only, or both, because you should address the person in exactly that way, and put their title of Mr. (*Gospodin*), Mrs. (*Gospod-a*)in front of it. In practice, the proper way to address Mrs. Mila Horvat would be "Mrs. Horvat" if she introduced herself by surname only, "Mrs. Mila Horvat" if she said both given name and surname, or "Mrs. Mila" if she just used her given name.

One more example: neighbors greet and

1 小写字母；小写字体

address each other using *vi* plus "Mr." or "Mrs." It can carry on like this for years and would be extremely impolite to use *ti* on any occasion. Also, not only with children but also in a situation where a younger person is speaking to an older one, it is proper to use the formal form, and in such a relationship it is not realistic to expect an invitation to address your elder informally. With parents-in-law, formal address is obligatory for the son- or daughter-in-law. Of course grandparents, aunts, and cousins are addressed informally. In a shop, even one you have been to every day for years, you will always use "Mrs." (though it is not necessary to add her name or surname), although the topics you discuss with such a lady may not be so formal.

The rules and situations above do not apply to the student population, who use informal address from the outset[1]. At the office, it is standard practice to approach your colleagues (regardless of level) initially with formal address, but within a matter of days this will become more relaxed. The important thing is to show good manners by starting properly.

[1] 开始；开端

WHERE TO MEET PEOPLE

It would be untrue to say that Croatians do not go out much, but bars or coffee shops are not places to meet people, in particular if you are alone. If someone is alone in a coffee shop it means they are there for refreshment[1] or to read newspapers, personal documents, or the like, and not to strike up a conversation with strangers.

A good place to meet people is the workplace. Accept invitations for coffee with colleagues. Other useful places are clubs, such as the Croatian-American Society, the Rotary Club, the Croatian-British Society, or similar associations for foreigners, or embassy events. If you are traveling with your family, this can help a lot: children playing in the park together are a great icebreaker[2].

In general it is unlikely that you'll be invited in for coffee with your neighbor, but small things like helping in some way, such as offering to carry shopping bags, can sometimes open doors.

1 点心；起提神作用的东西
2 破冰者；使谈话（或讨论、会议、社会活动等）活跃起来的言语（或事物）

STARTING A CONVERSATION

Croatian people are talkative. You will see that a Croat talks with hands, face, and body, not just the mouth—and don't be surprised at how noisy they can be, particularly in the south, where the mentality is characteristically Mediterranean.

Croatians are aware that few other people speak their language, and have no expectations that a foreigner will learn it unless planning to stay for a lifetime, but it is worth trying to learn a few basic phrases—this will help to break the ice and show that you respect the country. Middleclass and educated people speak at least two foreign languages, and one will certainly be English, but you might get into minor difficulties at the coast, where Italian is more common. Older people will probably know German or French.

Among the most common topics are family and children—since the family is so important people like to talk about simple things such as school, kindergarten, home life, domestic upsets, and the like. Another favorite topic, although almost every travel guide will advise you to refrain from discussing it, is politics: Croats very often complain about the state of things, but do not seem to realize that civil society is in their hands (though you would be best advised not to tell them this, at least not on first meeting). You should expect to be asked your views about the Homeland War and the Serbs. This is a tricky one, so be careful: as previously noted, the diplomatic response is to say that your knowledge is not sufficient and ask those present to give you some information about everything that happened. This is certainly the wisest approach if you are new in the country and among unfamiliar people.

Croats like jokes and humor: use these as an opportunity for talking, and don't hesitate to tell a good joke at the table. Croats don't eat in silence; they love long meals and cheerful company.

People will probably ask you about the purpose of your visit, your impressions, and the place where you are staying. Bear in mind that what is cheap or easily affordable to you is not so for many Croatians, so one of the topics will be the price of food and living costs.

One of the best topics is sports. Croatians are crazy about football, tennis, and skiing. If you come from a football-playing country, it is a good idea to inform yourself about Croats who play or have played for foreign teams, such as **Dado Prso**, recently at Glasgow Rangers[1], or the Brazilian-born Croatian international **Eduardo da Silva**, who moved from Dinamo Zagreb to Arsenal[2].

1 （苏格兰）格拉斯哥流浪者足球俱乐部，1872 年成立，球队主场位于格拉斯哥西南部的埃布罗克斯球场；是世界上著名的老字号球队，多次获得国内和欧洲联赛的冠军

2 阿森纳足球俱乐部，1886 年由一批热爱足球的皇家武器厂工人创立，主球场位于酋长球场；经过一百多年的努力，其成为英格兰最著名、最老牌的足坛劲旅之一，并已经成长为世界 8 大俱乐部之一

达多・普尔绍 (Dado Pršo, 1974-)

克罗地亚前足球运动员，早年在低组别俱乐部，后加盟摩纳哥及苏格兰班霸格拉斯哥流浪者，是一名大器晚成的足球运动员，他于 2007 年夏季宣布退役。

爱德华多・达席尔瓦 (Eduardo da Silva, 1983-)

1983 年生于巴西里约热内卢，2002 年获得克罗地亚国籍并加盟克罗地亚国家队，后转会阿森纳队，2010 年转会到顿涅茨克矿工足球俱乐部。

INVITATIONS

It is very likely that at some point you will be invited for a drink. In most cases this will be coffee, and you will be taken to some city coffee shop where people come and go all day long. Such an invitation might come during the lunch break or after work. Accept it, and rest assured that the person who invited you will pay. It would be polite to return the invitation for coffee, provided you wish to maintain the relationship. If you are not interested in continuing the relationship, just find an excuse for not going and don't invite them for a drink: everyone will understand the message.

If you find yourself in a pub and rounds are being bought, offer to buy a round yourself.

Invitations for lunch or dinner in a restaurant have a special message: they are part of business etiquette[1] or represent a show of affection. It is not common to have a meal together unless you have some serious intentions or want to show particular respect or gratitude on a special occasion. The expense of such a meal is always borne by the person extending the invitation.

1 礼节，礼仪

Invitations Home

An invitation to someone's home means that a relationship has reached a more intimate plane. If the invitation is for coffee, the timing may be fairly relaxed and no special gifts are needed, but do bring something, such as candies or nice fruit. If your host invites you for a meal, the time will be clearly stated and you are expected to come around fifteen minutes later (the so-called "academic quarter"), but not to delay your arrival by more than thirty minutes. You should bring your host a really good present, such as flowers (but not an even number, and never chrysanthemums[1] as they are for funerals and All Saints' Day), an expensive box of chocolates, and a bottle of fine wine or brandy. If you know there are children in the household, bring some candies for them too.

Taking your shoes off at the door is not common in Croatia, unless the family has a baby that has just started to crawl, in which case you might be asked to put on slippers which they will offer you on arrival.

The evening will start with *rakija*—homemade

1 菊花

brandy—and it will be appreciated if you give a toast in Croatian. The word to use is "*Uzdravlje*" ("To your health!") or "*Živjeliivjeli*" ("Long life!").

Don't just sit, as there may be a table plan, but if not you'll be asked to sit anywhere you like.

Short and Sweet

Don't take it amiss[1] if your host says "Sit!" to you, rather than "Please sit down." That's typically Croatian: abrupt, but hospitable.

It is most likely that the meal will consist of a starter, a soup, a main dish, and a dessert, and be rounded off with a *digestif*[2] and coffee. If you are a vegetarian, or have a special dietary[3] requirement, feel free to mention this in a gentle way in advance so that your host can prepare something appropriate. Croatians want to give their guests the best they have, and there is a proverb that says that a guest is a king, so you should bring a hearty appetite with you and try to finish what is put before you. It is impolite to come for dinner and then leave a full plate or only eat a little.

Elbows on the table are not a taboo any more,

1 错误地
2 餐后酒；助消化饮料
3 饮食的，饭食的

but if you are surrounded by older people, or if the occasion is official and important for your business career, it is wise to pay attention to that detail also and keep your hands below the table when not eating. It is a good idea to propose a toast to your hosts and thank them for the invitation—this will be appreciated. If you are a man, and there are women around the table, you should offer from time to time to pour them some water or wine—this will gain you marks for good manners!

In total, dinner starts around 7:00 or 8:00 p.m. and lasts two to three hours. Lunch timing can vary, but the biggest honor is to be invited for Sunday lunch, considered to be the most important meal of the week.

After being at someone's house, you are expected to return the invitation, though this can be a meal in a restaurant, paid for by you, of course.

Chapter 05

DAILY LIFE

As we have seen, Croatians have a strong sense of family and belonging, and as a result daily life is very much ruled by the family and other close relationships. People don't like to work long hours, and prefer to spend time with their families. Even during working hours Croats will take short breaks to socialize with friends. In fact you might well wonder if these people ever do any work at all and if they aren't always on coffee breaks. There is more than a grain of truth in this view of Croatians: socializing is immensely important to them and for most, work comes after friends.

THE CROATIAN HOME

Croatian conservatism is manifested in the domestic sphere. "Men are people, while women are just women," says an old Croatian proverb. Though today many Croatian men help with washing, cleaning, cooking, and childcare, the woman is still expected to hold up "three corners of the house." Wives generally cook each evening for the next day, and dining out is a rarity for most families. However, young people working on their career and with no domestic obligations often eat out with friends and colleagues. People with families will go out for a meal on weekends or on special occasions.

Croatians do not get married particularly young, tending to finish university or training and find a job first, and many couples live together to "see how things go." When a baby comes along, they do get married, almost as a rule, because having a child outside marriage is not considered "acceptable," and illegitimate children, as well as their parents, could be exposed to some unpleasant questions or at the very least odd looks from their community.

THE DAILY ROUTINE

For most people, the day starts between 6:00 and 7:00 a.m. The working day for most people is from 8:00 or 9:00 a.m. until 4:00 or 5:00 p.m., although of course those who work in factories, bakeries, or newspaper kiosks[1] and the like start and finish earlier. Traveling to work can take up to an hour and a half in big cities, where traffic congestion means that using public transportation is a better solution than driving oneself.

School starts at 8:00 a.m. for the morning shift and at 1:00 p.m. for the afternoon shift. In most primary schools pupils study in the mornings only for the first few years, but older children and secondary school students change shift each week. Children can have one to three meals (breakfast, lunch, snack) at school for a very reasonable price, but the food is simple and there is no choice (there's no chance of getting a special diet if your child is vegetarian, diabetic, or has other health problems). School ends around 1:00 p.m. for the morning shift, and 7:00 p.m. for the afternoon shift. In the first three years of school, children

1 报摊，电话亭

can stay with their teacher until 4:30 p.m., and do homework while waiting for their parents to come to collect them. After the third year, there is no such possibility, and homework is done at home on their own. Croatian children attend at least two weekly after-school activities—generally language lessons, sports sessions, or drama, ballet, or other dance classes. These activities are reserved for the evening hours, and sometimes finish as late as 9:00 or 10:00 p.m. There is no school on Saturdays.

Croatians work on Saturdays if they are employed in industry, trade, construction, health services, or similar, and on Sundays if staffing the major shopping centers. Visiting these big centers, which have restaurants, children's playgrounds, and cinemas, is popular in winter and on weekends, when whole families come to do their weekly shopping and combine this with the entertainments offered there.

Younger people go to gyms and fitness clubs on evenings during the workweek, while those with children hardly find any free time between job, school, and after-school activities, especially if they cook supper at home. Eating out is quite expensive, and Croatians do not usually eat out during the workweek. They will not even go out for lunch, but prefer to order their food in the office or bring sandwiches, yogurt, and fruit from home. The larger companies have cafeterias on the premises, offering their employees subsidized[1] meals.

People dine late, usually not before 8:00 p.m. As working hours are getting longer, and the rhythm of life has changed from Communist times—when mothers would, without exception, cook a hot dinner each day — it is becoming more and more common for individual family members to come home and prepare a cold meal for themselves. Families with smaller children are still in the habit of sitting around the table and having supper together, as it is the only meal they can share on workdays.

On weekends people love to go out for lunch. Usually they join up with friends and family, and such meals take a few hours because they are an opportunity to catch up with all the news. It is also common to invite friends for a barbecue at your country house, or to go out for a picnic.

1 资助或补助

The cinema is quite popular, especially on weekends. Theaters, museums, art galleries, and concerts are the preserve of a certain minority.

HOUSING

Young people live with their parents for a long time, many of them into their thirties, as finding a job can be a huge challenge. Buying a place to live is not easy when costs are compared with income. Many people rent an apartment while trying to scrape together enough money to start to buy their own home. Prices vary depending on the area (*kvart* in Zagreb slang) and the age of the building, but the price range is from 1,500 to 4,000 euros per square meter. In the city centers people live in apartments, while in the outskirts you will find family houses. The hilly part of the Zagreb area and the slopes on the west side are more expensive, and where the wealthier people live. There you will see nineteenth-century houses with beautiful Art Nouveau architecture

and huge gardens, and modern villas with high-tech features such as twenty-four-hour surveillance[1] cameras and garages with remotely operated doors, also with gardens. However, these buildings are not walled in the Russian style; they stand next to other houses and blend into the landscape.

In the town center you will see imposing Art Nouveau apartment buildings (*secesija*) stretching along tree-lined avenues. Here, the size of the average apartment is about 2,150 square feet (200 sq. m), with ceilings more than ten feet (3 m) high, and several balconies. These were built during the Austro-Hungarian period; some are still occupied by the old families that have lived there for generations, alongside others that have been let by their owners as offices to companies attracted by their location and prestige. Typical examples can be found in Zagreb's Zrinjevac Square, Massarykova Street, and Ilica Street. The rent for such an apartment for use as business premises is a few thousand euros a month.

Comparing the rents charged for apartments with the rates and expenses incurred by ownership,

1 监督；监视

buying is a better option if you intend to stay for any length of time. The real estate business is flourishing on the coast, although local people do not like to see foreigners buying places and moving in with their families. This may seem xenophobic, but Croatians are proud of their coastline and many are against the law enabling foreigners to buy property.

The worst time to buy or rent is in the early fall, when prices are highest. For houses at the seaside this applies to the spring as well, but property prices do not change as much as seasonal rentals. Apartments for rent are mostly furnished, or at least semi-furnished. A good place to start your quest for an apartment or house is: www.prodaja-nekretnina.com.

Houses are stone-built in Dalmatia and Istria (on the coast), while in the mountain regions and in the river valleys they are made of oak or bricks. Don't be surprised to see red-brick houses with no insulation or plaster: many Croatians will build a big two- to three-story house, spending any spare money on extra space, rather than finish a smaller house from top to bottom. This is particularly the case in rural or suburban regions where parents and their married children live together in one house, each family having one floor.

Also, you'll be surprised at how loath Croatians are to decorate their windows as many other Europeans do—there are no candles, cute details, or fancy lamps, though the hospitality once you get inside is astonishing. Generally speaking, Croatians like to preserve the privacy of the home, teaching their children that what is said and done within their four walls has to stay there. Although you may not see much of their privacy, you will hear a lot—Croatians are noisy, temperamental[1], and prone to[2] use colorful language.

CHILDREN

A new baby is a huge event for the family. While the mother and baby are still at the hospital, the father of the newborn holds a big feast for his friends in a bar or at home, and organizes a similar party at his workplace for his colleagues. Then the child must be "seen and gifted"; in most cases a piece of gold jewelry or an even more valuable

1 喜怒无常的；性情的；
2 有……倾向的

sum of money is considered appropriate. The child is baptized, and to be asked to be a godfather or godmother is a very great honor, almost greater than being best man at a wedding. Godparents become members of the family: no birthday or any kind of family gathering or celebration takes place without them. They are given a special status, and are expected to take their responsibilities seriously.

Children are very important, and they are treated like small grown-ups, going to restaurants with parents from an early age. It would be hard to name a place where they would not be welcome. However, they are brought up with quite strict discipline, and are taught to respect their elders: their parents don't allow them to annoy other people by running noisily around or playing messy games in public areas or on public transportation. It is extremely impolite for a young person to be sitting on a tram or bus while an older person stands; even if the older person is only middle-aged, the youngster must offer his or her seat.

Even when they are teenagers children still have to follow the rules, and Scandinavian-style youth democracy is not practiced in Croatian schools. Of those planning to go on to further education, many young Croatians choose to stay at home and apply to their local university, so as to keep in touch with their parents. This way of doing things is rooted in the Croatian way of life and its basis of traditionally strong family ties. Also the economy is such that young people are often obliged to rely on the support of their family, even if neither party regards the arrangement as ideal.

Grandparenting is highly developed and widely practiced. Children do not usually go to a kindergarten until they are three, so Grandmother is worth her weight in gold. This is not just because babysitting is beyond the means of most people, but also because Croatians are very reluctant[1] to leave their children with strangers. Even "his" mother is not a good enough choice for many young women, who would rather give their own mothers this important assignment.

Women can take maternity leave for six months on a full salary. After six months they receive only 2,800 kuna[2]. Most women stay at

1 不情愿的；勉强的
2 库纳（克罗地亚流通货币）

home for one year and then go back to work. It is very rare for a mother of a six-month-old baby to return to work. The state has set up a special program to encourage people to procreate, but so far the associated measures and procedures have done little to increase the birthrate.

The national death rate still outstrips the birthrate, though that just about puts Croatia in line with the majority of European countries and their aging populations. Families with three or more children are rare in cities or among educated couples.

EDUCATION

The educational system in Croatia is undergoing change. The universities have adopted the European Bologna system[1], and their degrees are recognized in the EU. Primary school education is moving toward a minimum length of nine years instead of the current eight, but secondary school is still not compulsory. This puts Croatia among the countries with the shortest compulsory schooling in Europe, but the minister of education has introduced a new program according to which twelve years of

1 博洛尼亚进程，是 29 个欧洲国家于 1999 年在意大利博洛尼亚提出的欧洲高等教育改革计划，旨在整合欧盟的高教资源，打通教育体制；到 2010 年，欧洲“博洛尼亚进程”签约国中的任何一个国家的大学毕业生的毕业证书和成绩，都将获得其他签约国家的承认

education, primary and secondary, will soon be compulsory, in an attempt to improve the statistics that show that only 8 percent of Croatians are graduates. The current situation is in marked contrast to the fact that **Zagreb University** was founded as long ago as 1669.

Education in Croatia starts at primary school at the age of seven (a six-year-old may start, but must take some extra tests). Before primary school children must attend a so-called "small school" (*mala škola*), or kindergarten, where they have writing and language lessons, and learn generally how to behave

萨格勒布大学 (Zagreb University)

其前身是建于 1669 年的 Jesuit 学院。作为东南欧最古老的高等学府，萨格勒布大学是一所综合性大学，学科门类齐全，涵盖艺术、生物医学、工程学、人文、自然及社会科学等，是世界大学前五百强之一。目前共有 29 个院系、3 个艺术类学、1 个克罗地亚研究中心，提供学士、硕士和博士课程。萨大的所有院系中医学院、电子工程学院、机械工程和海军建筑学院最为著名，其中电子工程学院在巴尔干地区属最强。该校于 2001 年与中国人民大学恢复姐妹高校关系并签署合作协议。更多详情请参见 http://www.unizg.hr/

and to concentrate, in preparation for school.

Primary schools are mostly state-run but in Zagreb there are also a few private schools. Among Croatians, going to private school is not considered an educational advantage, but it does have snob value, so private-school pupils do not usually mix with those from state schools. It is also true that private schools, and in particular private secondary schools, are usually full of students who were not good enough to get into a good state secondary school with strict academic entry criteria, and therefore had to buy a place at a private school.

After primary school, at the age of fourteen, children either attend four years of academic grammar school, which prepares them for university, or three years of profession-specific vocational school. While the primary schools are all much the same (there are a few Rudolf Steiner schools[1], plus some doing Greek and Latin), the secondary schools offer a wide range of specialist options: from language, music, and dance, to math, economics, engineering, and arts and crafts.

By the age of eighteen, when secondary

[1] 华德福学校，由奥地利教育家鲁道夫·史代纳在1919年根据自创的人智学理论创建，是一种以人为本，注重身体和心灵整体健康和谐发展的全人教育，如今华德福教育已成为世界上规模最大、发展最快的、非宗教的独立教育运动，华德福学校遍布各大洲不同文化背景和社会价值观的国家

克罗地亚的大学

在克罗地亚，目前共有七所大学，分别是萨格勒布大学、普利特大学、里耶卡大学、札达尔大学、杜布罗夫尼克大学、奥西耶克大学和普拉大学；学校一般多使用克罗地亚语授课，英语授课的专业较少；目前在克罗地亚的中国留学生数目较少，且申请手续较为繁琐，但学费相比中国较为便宜。

school is finished, young Croatians can choose either to continue their education by attending university in Zagreb, Rijeka, Split, Zadar, Dubrovnik, or Osijek, or abroad, or to get a job. Often, graduates of vocational schools attend evening schools or courses later in life to improve their job prospects.

MILITARY SERVICE

Croatian men used to go into military service either after secondary school (at age eighteen) or on finishing university, but, as of January 2008, this is no longer compulsory, because the Croatian government aims to establish a purely professional army. Women can also serve in the army, but

[1] 无情的，残忍的

only as professional soldiers. They can also be pilots. The Croatian forces serving with NATO in Afghanistan include several women.

EMPLOYMENT

The Croatian unemployment rate in 2006 was 16 percent. The main problem is the mismatch between supply and demand. The greatest need is for IT and telecommunications engineers, mechanical engineers, electrical engineers, computer experts, chemists and pharmacists, sales managers, PR professionals, and marketing managers. Finance experts are also highly sought after. By contrast, there is a long line of unemployed lawyers, economists, teachers, and other professionals from the fields of the social science and the humanities.

A large number of the people who are now unemployed worked for decades in big companies during the Communist era. In the new era of open markets and capitalism, those giants either lost out to more competent companies or underwent ruthless[1] privatization processes, which left many employees with no income at the age of forty-plus, when it is hard to find a new job. One peculiarity of the Croatians we have seen is that they are not flexible when it comes to the workplace. For instance, no one wants to work in the hospital in the undeveloped area of Vukovar in Slavonia, so Iraqi[1] and Lebanese[2] doctors can be found there. It is the same story in the less developed areas of Lika, Gorski Kotar, and even the islands. People would rather stay in Zagreb and have no work than uproot[3] themselves and move a fairly short distance east or south to make a living elsewhere.

Public sector jobs are considered desirable by those who crave security and are not ambitious: fixed working hours, free weekends, and guaranteed vacations are the advantages, but salaries are quite low. The private sector offers more money, but also demands more. Overtime is not usually paid, and staff turnover is high. Men are better paid than women in the same jobs; recent research showed the difference to be between 20 and 40 percent. They are more valued as employees (they don't need maternity leave), so

1 伊拉克人
2 黎巴嫩人
3 迫使某人离开出生地或定居处

women are at a disadvantage in the job market. Other research has shown that women are better workers, more loyal, and more responsible; also that they are the majority within the percentage of highly educated people in Croatia.

The best Internet sites for jobs are: www.posao.hr and www.moj-posao.net

SMOKING

Croatians smoke. In fact, the number of smokers is increasing, and even includes some primary school children. However, although smoking is far more socially acceptable in Croatia than elsewhere in Europe, in 2008 legislation was tabled to prohibit it in all public places, including restaurants and bars. At present, in big companies smoking is allowed in specially designated areas (usually a room or terrace), but not in the workplace itself.

Restaurants have small nonsmoking areas, but many bars and pubs do not. Cigarettes can be bought at kiosks marked "*Duhan*" and "*Tisak*" and in all shops. It is illegal to sell cigarettes to anyone below the age of eighteen.

Chapter 06

TIME OUT

You will often hear the older generation complaining about how much life has changed—how people talk and socialize less than they used to, how they work much more, how children today are left alone at home for hours—and it is quite true. A few decades ago employees in stateowned companies observed a sedate[1] rhythm: work was from 8:00 a.m. to 4:00 p.m., with weekends always free for family and friends. Things are different for young Croatians today. If they are career-minded and want to make good money, they work long hours during the day, and in the evenings too. When they are free, however, they like to divide their time between friends, family and sports,

[1] 镇定的，不慌不忙的

[1] 远足，短途旅行

eating together, and going on excursions[1] if the weather is good.

Having a weekend house by the sea or in the countryside is a great advantage, and everyone who can afford it does so. It functions as a second home for the family: many have gardens with flowers, small pools, and often a piece of land for outdoor play, and is a place where friends are invited for barbecues. Those who are not so lucky take their children to the city parks—it's almost a rule to have a Sunday afternoon walk with an ice cream or a Saturday morning stroll in the city center. Singles meet for coffee at their local coffee shops or city center venues. Going to the cinema is a popular evening activity, especially on weekends. Saturday and Sunday morning shows are for children. Tickets can be purchased over the Internet. Dinner at home with friends is also popular on Saturday evenings.

Make a good Croatian friend, and you, as a visitor, will be invited to join in. Also, if your family is in Croatia with you, this will help to break the ice and make more friends—family life is important for Croats, and you might well be invited, along with your children, to join another family for an afternoon picnic and games.

SHOPPING FOR PLEASURE

In Yugoslavia times, a few local factories produced the great majority of goods and there was little consumer choice. From the late 1990s, shopping centers started to mushroom and a new leisure-time pursuit was discovered. Today families visit modern shopping centers, complete with coffee bars and restaurants, playgrounds, spa centers, and cinemas, and spend whole Saturdays or Sundays there. The trend is more noticeable on winter days when the weather is too cold to be out of doors.

While main street shops are open from Monday to Friday, 8:00 a.m. to 8:00 p.m., shopping centers are open on weekends too, mostly until 9:00 p.m.

Croatians buy on credit: American Express[1], Diners[2], Master[3], and Visa[4] cards—all are accepted. If you have the misfortune to lose your credit card, call your provider's customer service number immediately to block the account.

EATING AND DRINKING

Regional Cuisine

Although a small country, Croatia offers a great diversity for food lovers. Its three different landscapes—continental, mountainous, and Mediterranean—provide a wide variety of regional foods. The local cuisine is further enriched by different culinary[5] influences and traditions—central European, Mediterranean, and Ottoman. Also, Croatia grows no genetically modified crops, and, in contrast to more developed economies, its food is produced on small farms with little use of chemicals.

1 美国运通，1850年由三家快递公司合并而成，总部设在美国纽约；美国运通旅游有关服务，美国运通财务顾问及美国运通银行是其三大主要运营机构，是国际上最大的旅游服务及综合性财务、金融投资及信息处理的环球公司，在信用卡、旅行支票、旅游、财务计划及国际银行业占领先地位

2 大莱卡，1950年由创业者Frank MC Mamaca创办，他推出了世界上第一张塑料付款卡，1981年美国最大的零售银行，即花旗银行的控股公司——花旗公司接受了大莱卡的塑料卡，现在世界范围内通用；该公司通过大莱现金兑换网络与ATM网络之间所形成互惠协议，从而集中加强了其在国际间市场上的地位

3 万事达卡，1966年在纽约成立；向全球消费者提供金融支付服务，包括针对支付行业的支付加盟、处理中心及顾问服务等，是国际知名的支付公司

4 维萨卡，是一个信用卡品牌，于1976开始向外发行，其前身由美洲银行所发行的Bank Americard；目前是由位于美国加利福尼亚州圣弗朗西斯科市的Visa国际组织负责经营和管理，国际著名银行卡品牌

5 厨房的；烹调用的

Istria and Kvarner have marketed and branded their own products and cuisines, and although these are not necessarily any better than other regional foods, they are certainly the best known—Istrian in particular. They use seasonal fare[1] characteristic of their climate, such as truffles[2], asparagus[3], fish, wild game, and olive oil, to make a combination of honest peasant food and good Mediterranean cuisine.

Truffle festivals (Istrian truffles feature in the *Guinness World Records*[4]), wine shows, asparagus days, olive oil competitions, cherry days, chestnut festivals, and the Kvarner scampi[5] season are just some of the activities organized for tourists—don't miss an opportunity to go along and taste. The Istrians also put a great deal of effort into promoting traditional and almost forgotten dishes from the inner parts of the Istrian Peninsula. The weekends see regular dinner or lunch guests from Italy, who love both the food and the stylish

1 伙食，食材
2 松露，又名块菌，是生长于地下的食用菌，有“餐桌上的钻石”的美誉，欧洲人将其与鱼子酱、鹅肝并称为“世界三大珍肴”
3 芦笋；龙须菜
4 吉尼斯世界纪录，第一次是在1954由著名的吉尼斯酿酒厂出版，该书作者是麦克沃特孪生兄弟；经过几十年的发展，该记录现共分为十二大类，包括人类、动植物等
5 ［无脊椎］挪威海螯虾

1 酒馆，小旅店
2 母羊
3 酸豆
4 迷迭香
5 薰衣草
6 鼠尾草
7 无花果
8 完全的；彻底的；货真价实的
9 ［动］食肉动物
10 烘肉卷
11 意大利乳清干酪

decoration of the Istrian taverns[1] and restaurants.

Dalmatian cuisine is considered the healthiest: olive oil, vegetables, fish, seafood, and red wine are the basic ingredients. Lamb, ewe[2]'s milk cheese, capers[3], olives, tomatoes, and spices such as rosemary[4], lavender[5], and sage[6], with figs[7] for dessert, complete the menu. Dalmatians live the longest, according to statistics, and that may be due partly to diet but also to the rhythm of life, which is more relaxed than further inland.

For out-and-out[8] carnivores[9], Slavonia is the kingdom: the food there is strong and spicy, the variety of sauces and roast meatloaves[10] is impressive, the wine is white, the brandies plentiful, and the women are celebrated for the pastries they bake. Just one look at the people there tells you they eat well: their cheeks are agreeably plump and rosy.

In Zagreb you can find a bit of everything: from ricotta[11] and white cheese with cream and corn bread (you can buy everything from local women at the fruit and vegetable market), through specialist fish restaurants and steak houses to elegant French and Italian establishments.

Dining Out

When visiting a local bistro[1], steak house, or tavern, you choose your own table. The menu is sometimes under glass at the entrance, but in most cases you'll have to go inside to see what's on offer. In classier places, booking by phone is welcomed, and a waiter will show you to your reserved table. The menu is almost always translated into English; prices are in kuna with VAT indicated ("PDV" in Croatian).

One potentially disappointing aspect of dining out is the general standard of service in restaurants and bars, and the lack of charm or friendliness on the part of the staff. Sometimes it can be quite a while before the waiter comes to your table to take your order, and when he does he may show little enthusiasm for his work. To put it bluntly[2], service can be slow and leave much to be desired in terms of effort. This is all the more unexpected because the ordinary people you meet on the

[1] 小酒馆
[2] 坦率地，直率地

[1] 卑屈的；过分顺从的

street are generally very friendly and hospitable. This attitude—a legacy from Yugoslavia times, when salaries were guaranteed and jobs were steady—shows that the country has some work to do to ensure the proper training of those working in the hospitality industry. They have yet to learn that being helpful does not compromise one's dignity, and that serving others does not mean that one is being servile[1].

Croats love both to eat and to cook. Eating out is popular among those who can afford it, but a good homemade lunch is still greatly appreciated at all levels of society. To be invited for such an occasion shows that your host particularly respects you, and the invitation should be treated accordingly. Croatians take their time over meals, not because there are too many courses but because they enjoy the food, talk at length, and don't hesitate to help themselves to more if they want it. A Croatian proverb says, "What's on the table is free," meaning that no one will be watching what you are eating or will mind if you help yourself to some more. Rather, they will welcome

a hearty appetite and appreciate spontaneous behavior at the table.

One authentic dish that you should try if you go to a restaurant is *peka*, which is meat (such as veal or goat) or seafood (such as fish or octopus[1]) cooked under hot ashes in a kind of casserole[2] dish. Bear in mind that this takes two or three hours to prepare and cook, and sometimes has to be ordered in advance, but the taste is splendid. Then there is *pršut* (cured ham), *kulen* (spicy sausage), Pag cheese, Livno cheese, *buzara* (a typical sauce in which scampi and shells are prepared), *brodet* (Croatian fish stew), rotisserie[3] meat (in particular goat or sheep), and *pasticada* (veal with a delicious spicy sauce and homemade gnocchi[4]). Inland, as well as *kulen*, try *lički lonac* (pork in shredded sauerkraut) and *sarma*, the traditional dish for New Year's lunch. Indigenous sweets are *štrukli* (pastry filled with fresh cheese, baked, and then roasted) and *kroštule* (long pieces of dough fried in boiling oil).

Drink

Drinking wine is also common during the day.

1 章鱼
2 砂锅菜；焙菜
3 烤肉店，烤肉铺
4 （面粉或马铃薯做的）团子

1 香草味的；香子兰，香草

Usually this will be just a glass of wine, unless it is a business lunch, when there will be a variety of bottles on the table to suit all tastes and accompany all dishes. Croats drink both white and red wine; red is characteristic of Dalmatia and the coast, whereas white is continental. Indigenous Croatian wines are Marăstina, Teran, Babić, Postup, Dingač, and Plavac. Try Graševina, Pošip, Rukatac, Žlahtina, Malvazija, and Vugava, if you prefer white. For dessert wine try Momjan, Muscat, or Prosek. Although wine goes with meals, Croats like beer too, local brands being Karlovačko, Ožujsko, and Pan.

Every meal, even a late dinner, finishes with coffee. Croatians make their coffee Italian-style: espresso, small or large macchiato, cappuccino, café latte. You can also order white coffee (coffee with milk), Irish coffee, chocolate or vanilla[1] Nescafe, or iced coffee. Drip brewed (filter) coffee is unobtainable in Croatia.

espresso

When it comes to tea, be ready for a surprise: should you ask for "English tea" you'll probably end up with Indian or Russian tea, with some milk alongside, but very often you'll be served black tea flavored with vanilla, or all kinds of fruits, with the Sir Winston label on it. Outside the Tea House in Zagreb, true English-style tea is a rarity in Croatia.

Black tea

ENTERTAINMENT AND NIGHTLIFE

Croatians above the age of about thirty-five rarely visit nightclubs or go to disco parties. The clientele[1] there is getting younger and younger: Croatian teenagers start going out to clubs when they are about fifteen. It is illegal to serve alcohol to those under eighteen. Smoking is permitted in clubs, as it is in most restaurants and taverns in the country.

During the summer, the coastal resorts offer some good venues for all-night parties: Aurora near Primošten (close to Split), or Hacienda, close to Šibenik (between Zadar and Split). In Zagreb, visit Aquarius or the BP Club for jazz, and for a beach party go to Zrće beach on the island of Pag. In Zadar, the Garden Club is owned by former UB40[2] members James Brown and Nick Colgan.

1 老主顾
2 英国乐队名，于 1978 年组建，其乐队成员都是来自于社会救济阵营；这支乐队的组成反映了工人阶级、黑人等下层劳动人民的街头文化，吸引了不满于现实社会的青年表现其政治愿望；代表作有 Labour of Love、Red Red Wine 等

TIPPING

Tipping is common in restaurants and coffee shops: tip around 10 percent of the total bill if the service has been good. Meal prices vary a lot, from 50 kuna per person to more than 800 kuna without wine. Credit cards are accepted at all but the cheapest establishments.

When you get a bill and give your credit card or money to the waiter, tell him discreetly[1] the sum you wish to pay, and he will understand that anything above what appears on the bill is a tip. In a coffee shop, the tip is usually given after a waiter brings you the change.

Taxis are expensive enough and tipping the driver is rare. Should you want to give a tip, it will be fine to add few more kuna on top of the bill or to round up an amount.

[1] 审慎的

There are cool clubs in every town, but these places are subject to trends, and locals will know what the most "in" place is at the moment, so ask them for advice.

SPORTS

First and foremost, Croatians love football. They are also interested in tennis, which is, however, still regarded as a sport for the wealthy, and all who can afford to do so play it, partly as a status symbol. Skiing and basketball are also popular, but not as popular as football and tennis.

Football—Nearly the Most Important Thing

Croats are crazy about football, and indeed say it is the second-most important thing in the world, after women. This drives most women crazy. Men meet in pubs to watch matches on TV, or invite a few friends over. Fights and conflicts are not rare, and fans can be quite dangerous. In the morning after a good match, men will discuss it in streetcars and on buses, analyzing the play. It's common to see grown men in good suits and ties talking passionately about football, like a bunch of kids.

DRESS

Croatians like to dress well, and enjoy shopping. This is a passion for many women, but young men are also often interested. Designer clothes are appreciated: in Croatia many people will judge you on your clothes and style, so it is

[1] 衣柜；行头

worth paying attention to this and having a few good-quality items in your wardrobe[1]. The Croats are not as formal as, say, the Germans, but elegance, refinement, and a modern style will certainly help you along in both business and private life.

WHAT TO SEE

Croatia is small but very diverse, offering mountain scenery, seaside resorts, and inland river retreats, as well as traditional culture and heritage monuments. Since everything is close (within five to six hours of driving, at most), weekends can be used to explore its natural beauties: the Plitvice Lakes, just forty-five minutes from Zagreb, are the premier national park in Croatia. Just a little way to the south lies the River Krka, with its gentle waterfalls. Mountain enthusiasts and walkers can enjoy the national parks of Risnjak, Paklenica, and Velebit— whose highest peak, Zavižan, rises 5,230 feet (1,594 m) above sea level. During the summer the Kornati archipelago, with a hundred and fifty uninhabited islands, is

a paradise for boaters. A similar oasis can be found on the island of Mljet, near Dubrovnik. Does the idea of playing golf surrounded by exotic animals—zebra, elephant, and giraffe—appeal? Then visit the Brijuni islands, near Pula, where Tito had his summer residence.

Top bird-watching spots are the Neretva River, near Dubrovnik, and Kopački rit, on the Danube in Slavonia. Both places offer accommodation and guided tours. Near Šibenik there is a falcon[1] center with three- to seven-day programs, offering you the opportunity to feed the birds, observe them, and help to tend those in the health center.

Full information and maps can be found at Croatian National Tourist Board offices. Call their tourist customer service (Croatian Angels) at 00 385 62 999 999. You can also visit www.croatia.hr for information and details about each travel destination, including telephone numbers.

The most important monuments and sites in Croatia are without doubt the old town of

1 猎鹰；隼

Dubrovnik, Diocletian's Palace in Split, the Arena in Pula, Šibenik Cathedral, and the town of Trogir. All these are listed by UNESCO as World Heritage Monuments.

FESTIVALS

The World Festival of Animated Film[1] has taken place in Zagreb in June or October for more than thirty years. Details can be found at www.ănimafest.hr.

In Šibenik each summer there is an International Children's Festival from mid-June to mid-July. The town becomes one big stage set: puppets, music, film, theater, and workshops are organized in the streets and on city squares. The Film Festival in Pula takes place in July in its huge Arena (the second-best preserved amphitheater[2] after the Roman Coliseum[3]), with seating for 7,000. In the 1960s, the Pula Film Festival[4] was regularly visited by Elizabeth Taylor, Orson Welles, and

1 萨格勒布国际动画电影节，1972年创办，是继法国安锡国际动画电影节后欧洲第二古老的动画节
2 圆形露天剧场
3 罗马斗兽场；罗马竞技场
4 普拉电影节。该电影节在普拉的圆形竞技场举行；它是世界上最大的6座罗马竞技场之一，同时也是世界上唯一完整保存了所有罗马建筑的竞技场，是克罗地亚最大且保存最好的历史遗址；普拉电影节在每年的夏天举行，同时还会有其他的活动，如音乐会、歌剧、芭蕾舞表演

Sophia Loren. Details can be found at www.pulafilmfestival.hr.

Dubrovnik is a member of the World Association of Festival Cities, and its Summer Festival holds an established position on the festival scene. The Festival has been running since 1950 and encompasses[1] theater, music, and dance. Shakespeare is always on the program; tickets can be bought via the Internet months in advance at www.dubrovnikfestival. hr. The Split Summer Festival (www.splitsko-ljeto.hr) also boasts a decades-long tradition, with opera, drama, music, and theater performed in the ancient open-air setting of Diocletian's Palace.

Another renowned film festival, younger than the one in Pula, is the Motovun Film Festival, which takes place in the medieval town of Motovun in the heart of the green Istrian Peninsula. During this five-day festival, people from all around the world come with their sleeping bags, turning the town into a film buffs[2] colony. Details can be found at www.motovun.filmfestival.com.

1 包含；包围
2 爱好者

Chapter

07 TRAVEL, HEALTH, & SAFETY

GETTING THERE

During the last few years, traveling to Croatia has become relatively easy. By air, there are two low-cost carriers operating from the UK—WizzAir[1] and Easy Jet[2]—and of course British Airways and Croatia Airlines. If you're traveling via Italy, you can combine air and sea: ferries[3] operate frequently from Venice, Ancona[4], Pescara[5], and

1 威兹航空公司，成立于2003年，是匈牙利一家廉价航空公司，总部设在布达佩斯

2 英国易捷航空公司，1995年由斯泰·利奥斯创立；是英国一家廉价航空公司，直销订票，服务简捷，不提供餐饮

3 渡轮；摆渡

4 安科纳（意大利东部港市）

5 佩斯卡拉（意大利东部港市）

Bari[1] to Split, Pula, Dubrovnik, and Zadar, and offer a good way to approach Croatia from the sea. Driving is also an option, and is ideal for adventurous travelers who have the time and want to enjoy the scenery. Croatia has very good highways and modern roads, making driving a pleasant experience.

Direct train lines connect Croatia with Austria, Switzerland, Germany, Hungary, Italy, Slovenia, Montenegro, and Serbia. If you will be coming from the UK by train, use the InterRail pass[2] that includes zone D. Travel from London will involve several changes, and information can be obtained at www.raileurope.co.uk or 08708 371 371. The domestic rail network is not very well developed, so you can reach Dubrovnik, for instance, by car, bus, boat, or plane, but not by rail.

Visitors from the EU, USA, Canada, Australia, and New Zealand do not need visas if they are staying for less than ninety days. But if you go from Split to Dubrovnik, you'll cross a small part of land around the town of Neum in the territory of Bosnia and Herzegovina, so you

1 巴里（意大利东南部海港）
2 欧洲火车联票

might be asked to show your passport (this applies to buses, cars, and boats). When you are already inside Croatia, a passport is not obligatory at all times, but some sort of photo ID should be in your pocket. The easiest solution may be to carry your driver's license.

Customs in Croatia are in line with the EU: foreign currency can be taken freely in and out of the country. In local currency (kuna), the law permits both residents and nonresidents to bring into or take out of the country any amount up to 15,000 kuna. For foreign currency (euros), the limit for both residents and nonresidents is 3,000 euros.

If you are planning to stay in Croatia for longer than ninety days, you will need a work or business permit. All information about residence and work permits can be obtained from the Croatian embassy in Washington (202 588 5899), and the consulates in Chicago (312 482 9902), Los Angeles (310 477 1009), New York (212 599 3066), Pittsburgh (412 843 0380), and Seattle (206 772 2968); the American embassy in Zagreb (385 1 6612 200); the Croatian embassy in London

(020 7387 2022); or the British embassy in Zagreb (385 1 6009 100).

TRANSPORTATION

There are no underground trains in Croatia, just buses, streetcars, overground trains, and, of course, taxis. The streetcar is a good way to get around Zagreb—natives will tell you that it is the fastest way to get anywhere, better than a car because the traffic is very heavy. Streetcars are frequent, but their timetabling is hardly Swiss. A ticket costs 7 kuna and is valid for one hour. Tickets can be bought on board (only the brand-new, very modern ones do not offer this option) or at kiosks labeled "*Tisak*" and "*Duhan*." In the main towns you can buy a daily ticket valid for all forms of transport. You can also buy a ticket using your cell phone: enter the letters ZG and send that text message to 8855. You'll get the e-ticket in a few seconds,

and it's valid for an hour. The price is 10 kuna, and the money is taken from your account at once.

Buses are a good option for intercity trips because train lines do not reach all towns and the difference in traveling time is huge. For instance, the journey from Zagreb to Split by train takes ten hours, but the same journey by bus takes only five—and by plane, forty-five minutes. Tickets for the city bus in Zagreb are the same as for the streetcar because the same company (ZET) provides both services.

Taxis are considered to be for the rich, and the service is great: there's no risk of having to wait more than a couple of minutes, no matter which part of Zagreb you are in and what time of day or night it is. The number to call is 970. It is important to note that you must pay in cash—taxis do not accept credit cards. Drivers will issue receipts on request. The meter is switched on for the journey, but longer distances such as from the airport to the city have a fixed price, and drivers will try to charge foreigners more than they would a local who knows the prices. If you need a taxi

from Zagreb airport to the town, the current price is between 150 and 200 kuna, maximum. In Dubrovnik and Split such a journey costs around 250 kuna.

Croatian cab drivers generally speak enough English to understand where you want to go, but it is worth having the address written on a piece of paper, in case of difficulty.

Between the coast and islands, domestic companies Jadrolinija (www.jadrolinija.hr) and SEM Marina (www.sem-marina.hr) operate daily ferry services and trips, all year-round. Timetables are displayed on their Web sites.

DRIVING

Croats are dynamic drivers, if not as obedient as Scandinavians, then perhaps more responsible than Italians. Pedestrians[1] are not as disciplined as in Switzerland or Germany, and cross the road more or less where they feel like. Croatia has zero tolerance of alcohol on the roads, so do not drink and drive. Speed limits are clearly indicated: 31.5 miles per hour (50 kmh) in built-up areas, 55.89

1 行人

miles per hour (90 kmh) outside built-up areas, 68.32 miles per hour (110 kmh) on divided highways (dual carriageways) unless otherwise stated, and 80.73 miles per hour (130 kmh) on the expressway. Use of a cell phone when driving is forbidden, lights must be turned on day and night (most rental cars have them set to switch on automatically with ignition), and seat belts must be fastened.

Should you bring your own car, you will need a valid driver's license, and vehicle registration and insurance documents. Should you consider renting a car, bear in mind that it is expensive: daily rental is about 500 kuna for a regular family car. This is the price without gas. Gas stations open from 7:00 a.m. to 7:00 p.m. (or 10:00 p.m. in summertime). Stations on international routes operate twenty-four hours.

库纳（克罗地亚流通货币）

DISABLED TRAVELERS

Croatia can be a very difficult place for disabled

people: stairs, toilets, and public buildings are rarely adapted to their needs, though there have been some good initiatives, such as opening a beach for disabled persons, and putting a special lift in front of the post office on Jurisićeva Street, in Zagreb. Also, in many places the standard door size does not allow for wheelchair access, so if necessary double-check this before confirming your accommodation.

MONEY

The easiest way to change money into kuna is to withdraw it from ATMs. They are easy to find in major cities and towns, and are placed at all arrival areas. If you are going to be in small towns and villages or on the islands, however, this is not the case, so you should change your currency at the airport, train station, or border crossing. Though Croats count almost everything in euros (hotel prices, apartment rentals, salaries, car costs, and so on), euros are accepted only in upscale hotels and at toll booths, so be sure to have some kuna with you at all times.

[1] 确定；查明
[2] 外币兑换所

Credit cards (American Express, Visa, Diners' Club, MasterCard,) are accepted in towns, but it is best to take cash when going to the hinterland or to the islands. Look at the stickers displayed at the entrances of restaurants and shops to ascertain[1] whether they will accept your card. It is a good idea to have at least two credit cards, because some places do not accept all types. Bank hours are: Monday to Friday, 8:00 a.m. to 8:00 p.m., Saturday 8:00 a.m. to 1:00 p.m.

You will notice that there are many bureaux de change[2] in every city: they have different exchange rates and fees, and if you are not familiar with the currency it is better to stick to ATMs. It is not permitted to change money on the street. If someone offers to do this, move away.

EMERGENCY TELEPHONE NUMBERS
Ambulance 94
Fire 93
Police 92

HEALTH

In an emergency, you can call an ambulance (see

above) or go directly to any city hospital—there are emergency services in all of them at all times. The best option is to ask around for the central hospital for your district. The doctors will generally speak English.

Croatia has a reasonably good national health service, but it is also possible to take out additional health insurance, through which you get some extra privileges and better prices for hospital services. There is a reciprocal[1] agreement with the UK, enabling British passport holders to get free hospital and dental treatment in Croatia.

If you want to avoid waiting by using one of Croatia's numerous private hospitals, you can expect to pay about 150 to 300 kuna per visit. The list of both hospitals and private clinics can be found at www.fivestars.hr.

Optical care is not free of charge: frames or lens replacements have to be paid for. A dentist will charge about 150 to 200 kuna for one filling. In recent years Croatia has become a dental tourism destination, and it appears that the same thing is happening with plastic surgery (http://www.

1 互惠的

treatmentabroad.net/cosmeticdentistry-abroad/croatia).

In Croatian the word for the pharmacy is *ljekana*, and here you can find medicines and some cosmetics. But Croatian pharmacies are reserved for prescription items and a few very special cosmetic products. Nonmedical products, such as cosmetics and film, which you would find in pharmacies in the USA, UK, France, or Belgium, can be bought at specialty stores, the most popular of which is the DM (Drogerie Markt)[1] chain.

SAFETY

Croatia has a low violent crime rate, but postwar depression has led to many job losses and a tough economic situation for some, so theft is not uncommon. Therefore it is wise not to leave anything in your car—not even a jacket or shopping bags. Also, watch your bag in the tram[2] and at the fruit and vegetable market. Apart from that, it is not dangerous to walk the streets late or stay out till the small hours.

Particularly on the coast, a woman sitting

1 欧洲药妆零售连锁企业，总部设在德国，经营的商品种类繁多，涵盖了营养保健品、卫生护理用品、家用物品、化妆品、婴幼儿用品、摄像器材和宠物食品等
2 电车轨道；煤车

on her own in a bar can attract a great deal of unwanted male attention. Croatian women are used to dealing with such behavior, but if you dislike it, move away and find a seat elsewhere. It is best to avoid getting involved in a verbal exchange with such men.

If you are passionate about walking in the countryside and exploring off the beaten track, watch closely for signs warning of minefields[1]. There are still some landmines left from the Homeland War in uninhabited areas such as Lika and Gorski Kotar, Slavonia, and wastelands on the island of Vis, but they are clearly marked and fenced off, and entry is forbidden.

WHERE TO STAY

Croatia has a limited range of luxury hotels and villas (in Zagreb, Dubrovnik, Opatija, and Poreč), but there are plenty of three-star hotels. The categorization system is not standardized, so some two-star hotels will be just fine for one or two nights and may be on the same level as three-star establishments elsewhere. Croatia also has

[1] 布雷区

apartments, rooms, and houses with full kitchens, which are highly recommended if you like a homelike atmosphere and prefer to prepare your own food. This kind of accommodation can be found at affordable prices, and the choice is huge.

Chapter

08

BUSINESS BRIEFING

THE BUSINESS CULTURE

The changes that Croatia has undergone since the Communist era are perhaps most marked in the business sector. Croatia today has a service-based economy (67 percent). The industrial sector comes second (27 percent), with shipbuilding, the chemical industry, food processing, machine tools, and the plastics industry prevailing, while agriculture (the export of organic foods and products such as wines, olives, olive oil, and lavender[1]) represents only 6 percent. Tourism is the mainstay[2] of the service economy, with revenue of over seven billion euros. In 2006 the country was visited by ten million tourists, putting it firmly

[1] 薰衣草，干薰衣草花
[2] 支柱，中流砥柱

on the list of the world's most popular tourist destinations.

The transition from a centralized command economy to a free market, the strengthening of the entrepreneurial spirit, the growing importance of lifelong education, and the increasing ease with which people can change jobs are some of the upsides. More than 90 percent of the economy is made up of small and mediumsized enterprises. On the downside, there have been failures in the privatization process that started after the Homeland War of the mid-1990s. President Franjo Tudjman—whose credit for strategy and firmness[1] in time of war is beyond question for the whole nation—initiated the economic process that led to the so-called "privatization robbery," which left an army of middleaged people unemployed and made a very few people tremendously[2] rich. The postwar era proved highly lucrative[3] and favorable for some private interests, but as a result of poor management skills, a number of successful Croatian companies went bankrupt. Croatian society's deeply rooted nepotism[4] has also impeded

1 坚定；坚固
2 非常地；惊人地
3 有利可图的，赚钱的
4 裙带关系

free progress in the jobs market.

After Tudjman's death, the new government, headed by Ivica Račan, carried out a large number of structural reforms and in the year 2000 the country emerged from the recession. According to World Bank statistics for 2006, Croatian GDP per capita is US $13,200, inflation is 3.3 percent, and the labor force is 1.72 million (out of a total of 4.4 million people). The average time required to start a business is as much as forty-nine days, owing to slow administration, a poor judicial system, and political corruption. The World Bank's main concern was Croatia's external debt.

After the Second World War Croatia had a traditional economy dominated by agriculture (more than 50 percent of the population were peasants), but in the late 1940s and early 1950s under Tito a rapid industrialization process began, with tourism taking off in 1965. Today, the rural population is 25 percent of the total, with 75 percent living in urban areas.

[1] 综合性大企业

Working in a public company provides Croatians with greater security but a smaller income. Working hours are fixed, and weekends and three to four weeks of summer vacation are guaranteed. Hierarchy is vertical, rules are strict, and working procedures do not change much.

The private sector is riskier: contracts are shorter—starting with three months, then one to three years, depending on the company, before a permanent position is confirmed. Overtime goes without saying. Private companies expect you to work long hours, but your contract will rarely include any compensation (extra payment, days off, or bonus payments). The reporting structure tends to be more horizontal, superiors are addressed more informally, and management changes are frequent. However, despite the element of insecurity, private companies offer their employees the opportunity to earn more, to get extra training, and to upgrade their skills.

Beside the private corporations, there are several Croatian businessmen who are building large conglomerates[1] and connecting companies by merging their interests in different industries. There are many more small, family-run firms employing just a few people and barely surviving from month to month. Many people made the decision to go it alone in the belief that they would at least be their own boss, even if, to begin with, the money might not be too impressive. This is a consequence of the widely held idea that employees are not paid enough or appreciated for the work that they do.

One of the downsides of Croatian business is the excessive paperwork, particularly in the public sector. Should you plan to start a company in Croatia, get ready for never-ending administration: it is not going to be a two-day job or one-stop procedure!

THE WORKFORCE

As we have seen, Croats are still generally unwilling to move around the country in order to get a better job, but this situation is changing with the younger generation. Of the 4.4 million inhabitants of Croatia, only 1.72 million work, so

1 冷淡；漠不关心
2 漫不经心

taxes are high. Education is another problem: only 8 percent reach higher education. On the other hand, in unskilled working environments (such as in construction, cleaning, or "dirty" jobs), you will find people from Bosnia or Albania, because many Croats refuse to do such work. But Croats are in general good workers, even if they don't perhaps match up to the workaholic standards of the Japanese or the punctuality and precision of the Germans. Some Mediterranean nonchalance[1] and casualness[2] is part of their mentality, and the workplace must be an enjoyable and pleasant place if the company wants to encourage their loyalty. Recommendations or connections help a great deal in all areas of business life. In Croatia, who you know is still more important than what you know.

Trade unions in Croatia exist, but almost exclusively in the public sector, so employees in private firms have no institution behind them to protect and assert their rights. The teachers' unions are among the strongest, but they are divided and each represents a different group of employees, inevitably lessening their overall strength. Some companies, such as the big shipyards, and the milk producers, have their trade unions, but their influence is limited. It is clear that there is a long way to go before people understand the importance of trade unions and the need to engage personally in protecting and fighting for their rights.

SETTING UP A MEETING

Be aware that getting to meet a decision maker is not easy, and that the relevant person's name is unlikely to be apparent from the company's organizational chart. This is because positions and responsibilities are for the most part based on personal alliances between people who hold certain positions, and sometimes it happens that the key person appears to have less influence than is in fact the case. It is therefore a good idea to ask around before setting up a meeting to discover just who is who in the company, and who is the best person to contact. Don't underestimate the time needed for this pre-visit work: knocking on the wrong door can block your chance of setting up a deal, so making personal contact with people who have some knowledge or experience with a company you are interested in could be crucial. Remember that in Croatia much of the real work takes place at dinners, social events, and other gatherings of key personnel. Recommendations are a golden key, whether you are looking for a job or have a business offer to make. Identifying the right contact is extremely important, as is timing.

Generally, the period from September (check the date when school starts) until May is a good time for negotiating or finding a job, with the exception of mid-December till late January—the Christmas, New Year, and skiing season. From May, people are starting to wind down toward their summer vacations, and by June it is already almost too late to start any serious project because summer relaxation has truly set in. So don't be surprised if your contact (particularly in a public service or state company) suggests that you send in your papers and arrange a meeting in September.

Suggesting a meeting on a Friday afternoon will not be viewed kindly: Tuesday to Friday mornings are best. On working days, in private companies, meetings can be scheduled for between 8:30 a.m. and at least 3:00 p.m. or, in most cases, as late as 5:00 p.m. In public companies the rules are more rigid: meetings take place between 10:00 a.m. and 2:00 p.m. at the latest.

Though the most desirable time for a vacation is mid-July to mid-August, it is a matter of agreement between you, your boss, and your colleagues when you take yours, and if one year you take leave in June and your colleague in July, the next year you may be expected to switch.

Croats like the telephone, and though it is important to make contact in writing, by letter or e-mail, a follow-up call should not be omitted. Though the Internet is very popular and people use it a lot in business, the personal touch given by a phone call still remains important for Croats, who like to hear a human voice. If you don't get an answer to your letter or e-mail, be persistent, and

don't hesitate to turn up in person at the company if necessary (this applies to smaller companies, where protocol is less formal, but you still have to be sure that your proposal is good enough). You should not have problems with language—most businesspeople speak English—but it would be a good idea when making a first approach to engage a translator to write your letter or e-mail in Croatian, and ask the company to note that further correspondence and conversations should be conducted in English.

MEETINGS

Croats pay a lot of attention to appearance and style. The Germanic style (that is, skirts for women and very formal classic suits for men) is not necessary: on the contrary, a fashionable but slightly informal style is welcomed. Men can wear a good linen suit in summer, with a smart pair of light shoes, an interesting tie, and a stylish watch. Women can wear attractive scarves, skirts, trousers, or fashionably cut dresses, with a good piece of jewelry and a really nice bag: all this can win you bonus points at the first meeting, which starts with handshakes and the exchange of business cards. This initial occasion is reserved for first impressions, relationship building, and watching for signals that indicate an ability to work well together. Conversation will be somewhere between small talk and commenting on the general situation, with some questions on business background, previous experiences, and insights you may have on certain business issues.

The meeting will be held in the office in most cases, but in some businesses, such as journalism, gastronomy[1], or fashion, a restaurant, quiet coffee bar, or—even better—a club may be suggested. If you are invited for a business lunch, you can take this as an expression of confidence: your counterpart obviously wants to give you significant time and attention. If you are a businesswoman, don't consider this improper: Croats like to show they are gentlemen, and they are usually more respectful with women in business than with male counterparts.

You will quickly see for yourself that Croats

1 美食学

1 优先于

like the personal touch, even in business, and almost any deal is based on a mixture of affection and competence; sometimes even the former takes precedence over[1] knowledge or ability. Be aware of that, and do not start a conversation with a cold, distant, or lofty attitude. Eye contact is important as well.

Be punctual for any meeting. Traffic can be very heavy, so leave extra time for delays. If you are going to take a taxi, which is a good idea particularly for a first visit, you will find the ordering service is well organized and you won't have to wait longer than two or three minutes for your cab to arrive. Call 970 from a landline or 01970 from a mobile.

It is considered polite to bring small gifts, such as well-made items with your company logo, or something characteristic of your country. Of course this depends on the purpose of your visit, but showing consideration in this way can help to get in touch with the necessary people, in particular if you are finding your way into a company's hierarchy. If you are given a present,

don't refuse it, however heavy it is: it indicates that you have won trust and that you are important. It will also pave the way for more close contact.

PRESENTATIONS

If you are scheduled to give a presentation, ask the company what equipment there will be at your disposal in the conference or meeting rooms. Some firms have top-notch[1] equipment but, to be sure, tell them what you need and ask if you should bring anything with you. Presentations should last no longer than twenty minutes. The discussion afterward will depend on the skills of the presenter, but might not produce much lively discussion, because people are generally still quite controlled in such situations.

Croats like colorful slides, and appreciate graphs and statistics, but the approach and tone of your presentation should be informal and friendly, with jokes and illustrative examples. In short, the American way—concise, precise, and vivid—will do well. Prepare material to hand out, including a few case studies.

1 最好的，卓越的

To warm up the audience, tell some anecdote from your business life—such as an amusing or odd experience from another presentation in another country—or simply go ahead with your impressions of the country. Of course, this will very much depend on the occasion, audience, and company you are in. In some contexts you will understand that the best way to start is just to introduce yourself and go ahead.

Your personality will be on trial, and you should be aware that people might look with greater interest at you than at your slides and charts. Body language is important, as well as eye contact. Reading the text, or sitting down during a presentation, will get you low marks, as will a superior or patronizing attitude.

NEGOTIATIONS

When it comes to negotiations, Croatians are flexible but not very quick to make decisions, so it will usually be necessary to have more than one meeting in order to reach an agreement. Sometimes this will be because the decision maker does not attend the meeting in person, and his delegate will report to him and get back to you, but in most cases time will be needed to digest the offer or proposal before making a decision. Negotiation in Croatia is thus hardly a one-step process. It takes some time and a little patience.

The structure of meetings is rarely formal: meetings are attended by no more than two or three people, each party has an opportunity to talk, and minutes are taken by one person who will write them up and send them by e-mail later that day. There will be an agenda, but the style is generally informal, and some small talk at the beginning is expected, though you should remember to address your counterparts formally (see page 76).

It is wise to put everything in writing for the sake of both sides and not to rely only on telephone conversations and face-to-face talks. Sending an e-mail in advance of the next meeting with points to discuss can help to keep the structure and focus. Also, this will ensure that the meeting is attended by people who have decision-making power on these issues, or who at least have some influence on the decision makers. Even in the course of negotiations, making private contacts and showing up at dinners that your counterpart is attending can help—if they see you at ease in familiar circles, you have a better chance of making a deal. Knowing the right people and visiting the right places can sometimes mean more than you might imagine.

Prices quoted in the first instance are generally negotiable. Bargaining is common and expected, unless your counterpart clearly indicates that he is making his last offer. Make sure you know whether or not VAT ("PDV" in Croatian) is included in the figures quoted. A self-confident, but not aggressive, attitude is respected. Your counterpart may be ready to concede reductions, but allowances must be made. Compensation can be of different kinds, so when preparing for financial negotiations think of a scale of possible equivalents that can be put into the equation.

When you reach the point where your business partner is serious about making a deal with you, an invitation for lunch is appropriate, and the gesture of a well-mannered person. Be careful about the venue—ask the secretary to recommend a convenient and suitable place: a quiet table with privacy to talk. Otherwise, your invitation could give the wrong impression.

CONTRACTS

When it comes to the contract, you will need both a notary and a lawyer. Before signing the papers, clarify the relevant responsibilities and obligations once again, insisting on assigning each task to a nominated person. In the end, even though most projects have a deadline, with clearly defined penalties for missing the date, you could still find yourself waiting. Croats tend to be flexible in the fulfillment of the contract. Adjustments and additions to contracts are common, and such interventions do not mean that parties do not understand each other or have poor communication.

[1] 耻辱；蒙羞

The legal system in Croatia is slow. Filing a lawsuit is easy enough, but getting a court decision takes time, so in some situations it is better to renegotiate terms than to sue the other party. Lawyers in Croatia are not expensive when their fees are compared with those charged in the USA and Western Europe.

MANAGING DISAGREEMENT

In Croatia, when authority was strictly enforced, many Croats can be slow to provide creative solutions, in particular if they are middle-aged or older. Young people, in contrast, appreciate being given the chance to use their own initiative by any manager who delegates responsibility to them. Even so, a certain level of supervision is required.

In the case of a problem with an employee, the boss should invite the person to his office for a private discussion of any mistakes and failings. Public humiliation[1] should be avoided. While money is a motivating factor for Croatian employees, human relationships and a good level of communication with managers can contribute even more to loyalty.

WOMEN IN BUSINESS

Women are generally better educated than men in Croatia, but most of the key positions are held by men. Even a woman in a high position will receive a lower salary than a male colleague. In business, women are usually treated by men with charm and style, but they might also be considered easier negotiators than men. Therefore, if a foreign woman has come to Croatia for business purposes, she will need to adopt a firm and confident attitude. A superior demeanor[1] will not win any favors, but she must keep on her toes[2]. Good advice to any woman planning to do business in Croatia is to be aware that feminine charms might bring some advantage, and that they should be judiciously[3] deployed.

OILING THE WHEELS

As mentioned above, knowing the right people is extremely important. In Croatia personal contacts are everything, whether you are applying for a job,

1 风度，举止
2 保持警觉
3 明智而审慎地

have a proposal on the table, or need entry to an important company. Here you are not necessarily expected to pay bribes or kickbacks[1], but you will certainly need the right connections.

According to Transparency International[2] CPI[3] 2007, Croatia was placed sixty-fourth in the total of 180 countries. The situation is improving year by year, but some neighboring countries have better positions: Slovenia was placed twenty-seventh, Hungary thirty-ninth. Austria was in 15th place.

You will also be aware that the competition is not about competence only. A word in the right ear about a favor done for a decision maker can help you win. Social skills and emotional intelligence are therefore at least as crucial as diligence[4], knowledge, persistence[5], and efficiency.

1 （不合法的）回扣，酬金
2 透明国际，全称为国际透明组织，1993 年由德国人彼得·艾根创办，总部设在德国柏林；该组织是一个非政府、非盈利、国际性的民间组织，以推动全球反腐败运动为己任，每年会公布清廉指数和腐败印象指数；今天已成为对腐败问题研究得最权威、最全面和最准确的国际性非政府组织，目前已在 90 多个国家成立了分会，研究数据被反复引用
3 腐败印象指数，又称年度清廉指数，由透明国际发布；以针对贪污的独立调查为基础，调查范围覆盖了 183 个国家和地区
4 勤奋，勤勉
5 坚持不懈；毅力

Chapter 09

COMMUNICATING

THE LANGUAGE

Croatian is a South Slavic language, and part of the Indo-European group[1]. Around 1500 BCE, a separate pre-Slavic language group formed within the Indo-European family and, following the migrations of Slavic tribes, these languages divided into East Slavic, West Slavic, and South Slavic. Croatian belongs to the last group, together with Slovenian, Serbian, Montenegrin, Bosnian, Macedonian[2], and Bulgarian.

The earliest form of the Croatian language, the so-called Old Church Slavic (or Old Slavic), from the ninth century CE, was the language of the first Slavic literacy and literature, associated

1 印欧语系，当代世界上分布区域最广的一个语系，包括梵语与欧洲的拉丁语、希腊语等
2 马其顿语

exclusively with Church ritual. Old Church Slavic used two scripts. The older script, used in Croatia, is known as Glagolitic[1] (*glagoljica*). The later script, known as Cyrillic[2] (*ćirilica*), continued in use, with minor changes and adjustments, in Serbia, Macedonia, and Bulgaria until the present day.

The oldest documents in the Croatian language are the Baska Tablet (*Bas´canska ploca*) from 1100, Istrian scripture (*Istarski razvod*) from 1275, and the Vinodol Code[3] (*Vinodolski zakonik*) from 1288.

The Latin alphabet was adopted in Croatia at the beginning of the fourteenth century, when the typical Croatian phonetic[4] forms *–ije* and *–je*, which are not found in other Slavic languages, took root.

In the nineteenth century the idea of language

[1] 格拉哥里字母，862–863 年间，圣西里尔为把圣经翻译成古教会斯拉夫语从而发明格拉哥里字母，是现存已知最古老的西里尔字母

[2] 斯拉夫字母，又称西里尔字母，相传由圣西里尔发明，后普遍在斯拉夫民族中使用；目前使用西里尔字母的文字不少是斯拉夫语族的语言，包括俄语、乌克兰语、卢森尼亚语、白俄罗斯语、保加利亚语、塞尔维亚语、马其顿语等

[3] 维诺多尔法则，世界上已知的克罗地亚最早且最为重要的法律文书，1288 年使用格拉哥里字母写就；与当时的罗马法律有很大不同，其中特别在于规定女性道德保护，不能在诉讼期间使用刑罚，被认为中世纪欧洲最为重要的法律文书之一，被至少翻成九种语言在欧洲流传

[4] 语音的，语音学的

reform initiated in Serbia by Vuk Karadžić took root within a group of Croatian linguists, who developed the project of forging one Serbian-Croatian language, involving the introduction into Croatian of unfamiliar structures, grammar, and stylistic forms.

With the formation of the First Yugoslavia in 1918, the King issued a law making it obligatory to use Serbian in the Croatian administration, schools, military, and judiciary. In spite of this, true integration of Serbian and Croatian was never successfully achieved because the historical differences were too great and too deeply rooted in the language structures.

In 1967 Croatian linguists published the "Declaration on the name and position of the Croatian language," which was strongly condemned by the Yugoslav authorities. *Croatian Orthography* by Babić, Finka, and Moguš followed in 1971; it was prohibited in Yugoslavia but the authors managed to print it in London, which acquired it a popular nickname—"Londoner." In 1974 the first Croatian grammar was published,

[1] 转变；转向
[2] 表示变音的

but was banned from schools and was first seen in public in 1979. The real linguistic turnaround[1] came in 1986 when Stjepan Babić wrote his book *Word Formation in Croatian: An Outline of Croatian Grammar*. In 1989 the parliament of the republic of Croatia initiated a correction of the constitution, replacing Serbian with Croatian as the official language of Croatia.

Written Croatian has several diacritical[2] marks, with "soft" and "hard" varieties. These are: Ć (soft), Č (hard Ć), Ž, Đ (soft), DŽ (hard Đ), and Š. Knowing which diacritical mark goes into which word is sometimes difficult even for natives, particularly if they are not university educated.

Diacritical mark	Pronunciation	Examples
Ć, Č	pronounced ch	as in approach
Š	pronounced sh	as in shame
Ž	pronounced zh	similar to measure
Đ , DŽ	pronounced j	as in jam

Croatian is a phonetic language, and words are pronounced as they are written, but the diacritical marks can cause you some problems at the beginning. The grammar is more complicated than English, while the syntax tends toward long sentences.

However, English is obligatory in elementary and secondary schools, as well as at university. Older Croats speak German, while along the coastline and on the islands people speak fluent Italian. In Zagreb and all big towns you should not have problems with communication: almost all service workers speak English. Just try to slow down and use simple words. On the coast, where Italian is more common, be prepared for some effort to make yourself understood, and use gestures. It will be greatly appreciated if you speak a few words of Croatian. Here are some basic words and phrases that might help you to get started:

Croatian	English
Dobar dan	Good day/Hello
Hvala	Thank you
Molim	Please
Dovid-enja	Good-bye
Oprostite	Excuse me
Govorite li engleski?	Do you speak English?

Swearing

Though good manners are appreciated, Croats swear quite heavily when they are in a relaxed mood or informal situation. The Virgin Mary, Christ, mother, and father feature prominently in the list of top swearwords. In Dalmatia, swearing is even more widespread than in Zagreb and its environs, though there are many people who use swearing to express their feelings, not to offend. So swearing is also used when people (mostly men) are in a very good mood and enjoying the company of their friends.

BODY LANGUAGE

Consistent with their openness, you'll find that Croats touch each other frequently, stand close to each other when talking, and greet each other by kissing once on each cheek (Serbs kiss three times)—but they really do kiss, by touching the cheeks with their lips, not just "air kissing." Older men will kiss a woman's hand, particularly in Zagreb, where a well-mannered person is said to be of the "Vienna school"—a carryover from the days of the Habsburg monarchy.

Croats use body language a great deal. For an outsider it can seem a bit over the top, particularly when a man and a woman are in conversation. Touching, hugging, caressing[1], standing close to another person, and smiling are normal, and people don't intend to cause offense if they invade your personal space more than you might expect.

People in Croatia have no problem with showing their emotions, and they are loud about expressing them. Also, if you are a woman and are smiled at by an unknown man on the street, don't treat it disdainfully[2]. If you feel good, return the smile; if it is not your day, just ignore it and walk on. A man's manners are closely observed by Croatian women: it is appreciated if he offers to take a woman's coat, carries her bags from the shops, opens the car door, holds the door for her at the entrance of a restaurant, pours her some water, or lights her cigarette. The man must always pay the bill if only the two of them are at the table.

There are certain hand gestures with a specific meaning: thumb and forefinger joined

1 爱抚
2 轻蔑地

to form a circle means "splendid" or "perfect". This gesture is used if, say, dinner is delicious, or if you feel great, or if someone looks really good in a special outfit. The thumbs-up sign has much the same meaning. The V-sign stands for victory and is connected to Homeland War issues. In traffic, the middle finger is a common way of communication between annoyed drivers. A raised thumb pointed backward means something is literally behind, or that something has passed, or is irrelevant. A forefinger pointing at the temple combined with twisting the hand from the wrist means that a person is crazy, but this is a rather childish gesture. Pulling down a lower eyelid with a forefinger means one is faking, pretending, or lying.

THE MEDIA

Television

Television is by far the most popular and most influential medium in Croatia. There are four main TV stations: HRT 1 and HRT 2, which

are state-owned, and RTL and Nova TV, representing the commercial sector. The output of HRT1 caters very much to the mainstream—news, educational programs, films, and documentaries—while HRT2 is oriented more toward sports, also showing British and American serials and the occasional film in the evenings. The commercial channels are aimed at a younger, trendier audience, with reality shows, celebrity coverage, and comment-laden[1] news programs. Beside these national broadcasters there are a number of local channels.

Radio

Croatia has nearly two hundred radio stations. State-owned HR1 and HR2 broadcast politics, news, sports, and entertainment. HR3 is reserved for a cultural agenda. Popular commercial stations are Otvoreni Radio, www.otvoreni.hr, and Radio 101, www.radio101.hr, which broadcast a mixture of British and American music and tend to take a more independent political line.

[1] 带有评论的

[1] 掺和，混合

The Press

Croatian magazines and newspapers are available at kiosks ("*Duhan*" or "*Tisak*"). The best-selling broadsheets are *Vecernji List* and *Jutarnji List*, both European-owned (Europapress Holding, owned by Austrian Styria). The third-best-selling daily is *Slobodna Dalmacija*, a local Dalmatian-owned newspaper that represents more conservative attitudes.

The daily newspaper *Vjesnik*, which for decades was read by intellectuals and well-educated people only, lost this status after the state was unable to continue to finance it. It had to enter the free market game, and in order to increase sales changed the content significantly but kept the tone and style from the old times.

Most weekly and monthly publications are also published by Europapress Holding. Among the most influential and best-selling political magazines are *Nacional* and *Globus*. Their main topics are economics and politics, with a small admix[1] of celebrity pages.

Women's magazines, such as *Cosmopolitan*, *Elle*,

Elle Décor, *Vanity Fair*, and the like can be found at kiosks.

The most popular tabloid[1] is *24 Hours*, a small-format newspaper that is given free of charge in streetcars in the afternoons; in the mornings you can buy it from newsdealers or at kiosks.

Generally, the Croatian press can be quite salacious[2], and porn magazines are sold openly to people aged over eighteen.

A good selection of European and British newspapers and magazines can be found in Algoritam, the biggest foreign bookshop in Zagreb (in the very center of the town). The larger "*Tisak*" kiosks also offer a respectable choice, usually only a day or two behind publication.

SERVICES

Telephone

The biggest telephone company in Croatia is T-Com, owned by the German company Deutsche Telecom, with about 80 percent market share and almost total control over landlines. They carry

1 小报
2 淫秽的，色情的

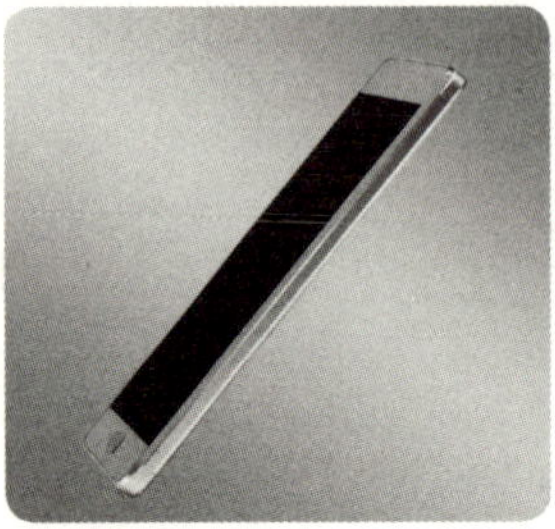

Internet and cell phone traffic as well, but apart from them there are also Iskon, Optima Telecom, and a few smaller companies.

Cell phones are very popular. Statistics show that each family has at least three mobile devices and even first-grade children carry them to school. Mobile signals (Croatia is on the GSM system) are provided by two big operators, VIP (Vodafone[1]) and T-Mobile[2] (a branch of T-Com) plus a few smaller operators. For detailed information visit www.vip.hr and www.t-mobile.hr. Any European cell phone will work from Croatia: only North Americans will find their handsets inactive. If you are staying longer buy a local SIM card to save money on roaming fees.

In hospitals, schools, and similar institutions you can find phone booths, as well as in all post offices, where you can either use a phone booth and pay cash to the clerk behind the window or buy a phone card (they have 25 to 500 units called *impuls*), which is recommended for international calls. A fifty-unit phone card (costing 50 kuna) is sufficient for a short international call. Small

1 沃达丰（英国电信企业）
2 德国电信公司

towns in the countryside will generally have phone booths. Don't call internationally from a hotel or hostel landline—this is very expensive. When calling internationally from Croatia, the prefix 00 is your international access code. The dialing code for Croatia is 00 385.

Mail

The Croatian mail services are reasonably cheap, and reliable. The offices can be recognized by their distinctive logo: a black trumpet on a yellow background. The same symbol is found on the yellow mailboxes on the streets. Depending on your needs, you can send a letter, package, or money using ordinary or priority postal service. Stamps for ordinary mail can be bought at tobacco kiosks (*Tisak* or *Duhan*).

Post offices also handle telegrams, faxes, utility bills, and currency exchange—make sure you are waiting in the right line.

Hrvatska pošta d.d.

If sent by the ordinary service, a letter or package takes two to three days at most to be delivered within Croatia. Across Europe it will take about a week to ten days. HP Express is quite a new postal service that comes to your home or office, picks the mail up, and guarantees delivery within twenty-four hours. Prices are moderate. FedEx, UPS, and DHL have offices around Croatia as well.

For mail sent across Croatia, the address should be written in the following way:

Horvat Ivan (surname followed by first name)
Vukovarska 23
10 000 Zagreb

It is important to include the five-digit postcode of the town or village. If you are not sure what it is, call the General Information Service on 988 and ask them for help, or visit http://www.poslovniforum.hr/postanski.asp. All additional information about postal services can be found on the Web site www.posta.hr.

Internet

Statistics show that more than 38 percent of Croats

use the Internet, mostly from home and the office, ranking the country with Spain, Portugal, the Czech Republic, Slovakia, and Poland. In terms of numbers, this percentage means that around one and a half million Croats have Internet access and use it. Seventy percent of total use is taken up by e-mail. Internet providers are T-Com, Iskon, Optima Telecom, and a few small companies.

Internet access can be found in Internet cafés at reasonable rates. Sometimes it is available in public libraries as well. Prices are charged by the hour or minute. As you travel further south and move away from bigger towns, Internet cafés are harder to find. Wi-Fi is available from such places as hotels, airports, and marinas[1] (a full list can be found at www.t-mobile.hr). Cards for Wireless Local Area Network are available at T-Mobile shops.

CONCLUSION

Whether your visit to Croatia is short or long, you will soon realize that Croatian people welcome a natural, open, human approach. You don't need

1 渡船码头

to be perfect, just straightforward. Be yourself and they will respond warmly.

The country is among the most prosperous in this part of Europe, and the process of transition will in time bring improvements in the areas of the judiciary and public administration, which are at the moment being reformed in accordance with European Union regulations. As the country prepares to enter the EU in 2009/10, the prospects for the near future are good.

With its beautiful coastline, unspoiled countryside, and organic food, the coming years promise much to both residents and visitors. *National Geographic Adventure* nominated Croatia as one of the top three countries for a vacation in 2006. It was also listed in the Lonely Planet directory of top ten destinations in the world in 2005. The travel industry, with its associated services, and the new technologies, are the most prosperous sectors in Croatia's economy, which is a good model for neighboring countries passing through a similar transition process.

Sometimes you may find the Croatian need to

talk a lot annoying, or that their tendency to show emotion by touching and encroaching on[1] your personal space is a bit much, but do not take this amiss[2]; it is well-meant. You may also come across varying attitudes and habits in different parts of the country due to different lifestyles, or diverging mind-sets, depending on which generation you are meeting. People in the big towns will have few prejudices and you'll get along with them easily. In smaller communities you'll experience the warmth characteristic of all village people, but their way of life, unchanged for decades, might well present a small challenge to your way of thinking. Along the coast you'll probably meet expressive and natural people whose outlook will surprise you if work and money are at the top of your priorities—they enjoy the modest, natural things of life, and prefer to spend time and laugh with their friends.

You are bound to experience some downsides, such as the dead hand of bureaucracy[3], when doing business in Croatia, and will come to learn a few tricks to help you cut through the red tape; but if you are prepared to deal with those issues, your

1 侵占
2 不对，不正常
3 官僚主义

time in Croatia should be a very happy one.

Many people from the UK, France, Italy, and Germany buy properties in Croatia and spend long periods of time there each year because the pace of life is slower, gentler, and less stressful than in Western Europe, making for a better quality of life all around. Though not all Croatians are happy about foreigners coming to live in their country, those who come with respect and understanding of the country's true values are warmly welcomed.

APPENDICES

PLACES

Adriatic Sea
亚得里亚海（位于意大利东海岸和巴尔干半岛之间，是地中海的一个大海湾）

Ancona
安科纳（意大利东部港市）

Apennine Peninsula
亚平宁半岛(现大部分在意大利境内，也称意大利半岛；是南欧三大岛之一)

Balkan Peninsula
巴尔干半岛（地处欧洲东南部，位于亚得里亚海和黑海之间，是南欧三大岛之一）

Bari
巴里（意大利东南部海港）

Belgrade
贝尔格莱德（塞尔维亚共和国首都）

Bulgaria
保加利亚(欧洲东南部国家）

Cape Savudrija
皮兰角（位于亚得里亚海的子海湾——皮兰湾域内，靠近斯洛文尼亚的皮兰市）

Carpathian

喀尔巴阡山脉的（位于欧洲中部。在多瑙河中游以北。全长1,450千米。西起奥地利与斯洛伐克边界多瑙河峡谷，向东呈弧形延伸，经波兰、乌克兰边境至罗马尼亚西南的多瑙河谷的铁门峡谷。）

Cres

茨雷斯岛(位于克罗地亚境内，亚得里亚海沿岸岛屿)

Dalmatia

达尔马提亚地区，包括亚得里亚海沿岸的达尔马提亚群岛和附近1,000多个小岛；总面积1.3万平方公里，其行政中心为斯普利特

Danube

多瑙河（发源于德国，流经奥地利等十个国家，后注入黑海，是欧洲第二大河流）

Dinara

迪纳拉山脉（地处欧洲东南部，为欧洲第四大山脉）

Dubrovnik

杜布罗夫尼克市(克罗地亚南部港市，濒临亚得里亚海)

Gorski Kotar

戈尔斯基科塔尔地区，以山区为主

Hague

海牙（荷兰西部城市，联合国国际法院所在地）

Hungary

匈牙利（欧洲中部国家）

Hvar

赫瓦尔岛，地处克罗地亚沿海达尔马提亚群岛，是沿岸最长的岛屿，靠近斯普利特的南部

Istria
伊斯特里亚（欧洲巴尔干半岛西北部的半岛）

Krk
克尔克岛(位于克罗地亚境内，地处亚得里亚海北部)

Kvarner
克瓦内尔(克瓦内尔海湾是亚得里亚海的一个子海湾，位于亚得里亚海的北部，以克尔克岛和茨雷斯岛为屏障)

Lika
利卡地区，位于克罗地亚中部

Lošinj
洛希尼岛，位于亚德里亚海北部，克瓦内尔湾内

Montenegro
黑山共和国（前南斯拉夫成员共和国）

protected national parks
国家公园（克罗地亚境内共有八座国家公园，依次是科纳提国家公园、里斯尼亚克国家公园、卡尔卡国家公园、帕克莱尼采国家公园、布里俄尼群岛国家公园、北韦莱比特国家公园、普利特维采湖区和姆列特国家公园）

Palagruža
帕拉格鲁扎群岛（克罗地亚境内群岛）

Pannonian
潘诺尼亚的（古罗马中欧省份，位于多瑙河和萨瓦河之间）

Pescara
佩斯卡拉（意大利东部港市）

Prevlaka
普雷夫拉卡岛（现属黑山共和国）

protectorate

保护国；摄政政体

Rab

拉布岛，位于达尔马提亚最北部分，著名的旅游胜地

Republic of Serbian Krajina

塞尔维亚克拉伊纳共和国（原克罗地亚克拉伊纳自治区，1991年宣布独立后控制了克罗地亚与波黑边境的塞族地区）

Rijeka

里耶卡市（克罗地亚境内的一座港口城市）

Romania

罗马尼亚（欧洲巴尔干半岛东北部国家）

Serbia

塞尔维亚（前南斯拉夫成员共和国）

Slovenia

斯洛文尼亚（前南斯拉夫成员共和国）

Split

斯普利特市，历史名城；克罗地亚第二大城市，是达尔马提亚地区第一大海港

Starigrad

斯塔里格勒（旧称Pharos），地处克罗地亚达尔马提亚地区斯普利特-达尔马提亚县赫瓦尔岛北侧，历史悠久，是欧洲最古老的城镇之一

Vis

维斯岛，地处克罗地亚亚得里亚海沿岸，位于达尔马提亚群岛外侧

Vukovar

武科瓦尔（克罗地亚东部边境城市）

Zadar

扎达尔市(克罗地亚西南部海港)

Zagreb

萨格勒布（克罗地亚首都，位于克罗地亚的西北部）

PEOPLE

Aleksander Karadordević (1806–1885)

塞尔维亚大公（1842–1858）。早年在俄军中服役。1842年被国民议会推举上台以代替被废黜的米哈伊洛·奥布雷诺维奇大公，开始卡拉乔尔杰维奇王朝在塞尔维亚公国的正式统治。对外政策动摇不定，或亲俄或亲奥；在1848–1849年革命中，未派军支援匈牙利的斯拉夫人；克里米亚战争中迫于奥、土压力，持中立立场。1858年12月被国民议会废黜，卡拉乔尔杰维奇王朝统治中断。

Ante Starčević (1823–1896)

安特·斯塔尔切维奇，克罗地亚政治家，被誉为“祖国之父”，克罗地亚民族解放运动领袖，现代克罗地亚国家肇建者

Bernie Ecclestone (1930–)

伯尼·埃克莱斯顿，F1控股公司的老板，持有F1赛事的商业经营权，被视为“F1赛车帝国的国王”，将F1赛车从最初的混乱不堪、经营惨淡的比赛项目，变成今天这样一个产值数十亿美元的王国

Dado Pršo (1974–)

达多·普尔绍，克罗地亚前足球运动员，早年在低组别俱乐部，后加盟摩纳哥及苏格兰班霸格拉斯哥流浪者，是一名大器晚成的足球运动员，他于2007年夏季宣布退役

Eduardo da Silva (1983–　)

爱德华多·达席尔瓦，1983年生于巴西里约热内卢，2002年获得克罗地亚国籍并加盟克罗地亚国家队，后转会阿森纳队，2010年转会到顿涅茨克矿工足球俱乐部

Emperor Constantine (272–337)

君士坦丁大帝，古罗马帝国统治者，君士坦丁大帝是古罗马第一位信奉基督教的皇帝，他于公元330年迁都至拜占庭，并改名君士坦丁堡；君士坦丁大帝颁布的一系列措施促进欧洲从奴隶社会向封建社会转变，史称“千古一帝”

Ferdinand Ⅰ (1549–1609)

斐迪南一世，托斯卡纳大公（1587年-1609年在位），在位期间与奥地利哈布斯堡王朝的统治者们保持良好关系，曾帮助奥地利抵挡奥斯曼帝国的进攻

Franjo Tudjman (1922–1999)

弗拉尼奥·图季曼博士，克罗地亚前总统，是1991年克罗地亚脱离南斯拉夫联盟独立战争的领袖

Goran Ivanišević (1971–　)

伊万尼塞维奇，克罗地亚著名网球男运动员，1971年出生于斯普利特，身高193cm，7岁便开始打网球，在2001年拿下温布尔登男单冠军，现居于蒙特卡罗

James Joyce (1882–1941)

詹姆斯·乔伊斯，爱尔兰作家、诗人，二十世纪最伟大的作家之一，后现代文学的奠基者之一。其代表作有短篇小说集《都柏林人》，长篇小说《尤利西斯》和《芬尼根的守灵夜》等，其作品及“意识流”思想对世界文坛影响巨大

John Malkovich (1953–　)

约翰·马尔科维奇，美国男演员、制片、导演和编剧，曾获第57、66两届奥斯卡最佳男配角奖，代表作有《推销员之死》和《心田深处》等

King Tomislav (about 880–928)

托米斯拉夫国王（925–928），托米斯拉夫是克罗地亚特尔皮米罗维奇王朝大公(910–925)，后成为克罗地亚的第一任国王(925–928)。

Louis II (1506–1526)

拉约什二世，弗拉迪斯拉斯二世的继承人，于1516年继位，1521年亲政；是亚盖隆王朝的匈牙利国王和波希米亚国王，1526年在第一次摩哈赤战役中战死

Miroslav Krleža (1893–1981)

克尔莱扎，克罗地亚小说家，剧作家，出身于萨格勒布市一资产阶级家庭，代表作有《加利齐亚》《果尔果达》《狼谷》以及《格列姆巴伊老爷们》《垂死挣扎》《丽达》三部曲和《阿雷特伊》等

Mussolini (1883–1945)

墨索里尼，意大利法西斯党首领及独裁者

Napoleon (1769–1821)

拿破仑，十九世纪著名军事家、政治家；曾执掌法兰西共和国，后创建法兰西第一帝国；执政期间，多次发动战争向外扩张，五破反法联盟，占领欧洲大片土地，建立了庞大的拿破仑帝国；后于1815年滑铁卢战争失败后，被流放至大西洋的圣赫勒拿岛，1821年在此病逝

Princess Caroline (1957–)

卡罗琳公主，摩纳哥大公主；是前摩纳哥国家元首——兰尼埃三世亲王与摩纳哥王妃——格雷丝·凯莉的长女。是现在位亲王阿尔贝二世的亲姐姐

Queen Teuta

托伊塔女王，古伊利里亚的女王，生活在公元前3世纪晚期，史称“海盗女王”；在她摄政期间，她的舰队掠夺罗马人的财物，射杀并羞辱罗马使节，罗马因此向伊利里亚宣战并赢得胜利；后在第二次马其顿战争中倒向马其顿，罗马和希腊联手从伊利里亚登陆，古伊利里亚就此覆灭

Sir Roger Moore (1927–)

罗杰·摩尔爵士，英国男演员，第三任007扮演者，是007扮演者中"年龄最大、任期最长"的邦德

Tito (1892–1980)

铁托，前南斯拉夫社会主义联邦共和国总统、南斯拉夫共产主义者联盟总书记、南斯拉夫人民军元帅；在二战中领导南斯拉夫人民进行反法西斯运动，做出重要的贡献；二战后坚持"南斯拉夫人的南斯拉夫"原则，与苏联关系破裂，危机重重，但铁托以强硬手段维护了南斯拉夫的统一

Tom Cruise (1962–)

汤姆·克鲁斯，美国男演员，电影制片人，曾获第47届和54届金球奖最佳男主角，代表作有《夜访吸血鬼》、《甜心先生》和《碟中谍》等

SOME FAMOUS CROATS

Juraj Julije Klović (1498–1578)

Dalmatian Renaissance illuminator, iniaturist, and painter who worked in Italy and was considered the greatest illuminator of the Italian High Renaissance. His reputation was such that El Greco painted his portrait twice, putting him in the company of Michelangelo, Titian, and Raphael in one of his paintings. He was given the nickname "Michelangelo of the miniature." Today the British Library has his twelve miniatures illustrating victories of the Emperor Charles V. Other miniatures can be found in Vatican Library, the New York Public Library, and national libraries in Vienna, Paris, and Munich. The City of Zagreb also has a collection of his works.

Faust Vrancić (1551–1617)

A humanist, philosopher, lexicographer, and inventor whose book *Machinae*

Novae (1595), containing forty large etchings showing fifty-six different machines and technical concepts, was quickly translated into Italian, French, and German. Among other subjects in this work, Vrančić examined Leonardo da Vinci's famous "Homo Volans" sketch, and presented his idea for a parachute. Twenty years later he implemented his ideas and made a parachute, which he tested by jumping from a tower in Venice in 1617. The event was later documented by John Wilkins, first secretary of the Royal Society in London.

Marin Getaldić (1568–1626)

A scientist who specialized in optics and mathematics and whose contributions to geometry (*Variorum Problematum Colletio*, 1607) were cited by Edmund Halley, of comet fame. Among his constructions was a parabolic mirror, now in the National Maritime Museum in London.

Josip Ruder Bosković (1711–87)

A physicist, astronomer, mathematician, and philosopher, famous for atomic theory. His work had a direct influence on Michael Faraday. In astronomy Bošković invented the first geometric procedure for determining the equator from a rotating planet. In 1753 he also discovered the absence of atmosphere on the moon. A moon crater was named after him in honor of his contributions to astronomy.

Nikola Tesla (1856–1943)

Inventor, physicist, mechanical engineer, and electrical engineer, known for revolutionary contributions to the discipline of electricity and magnetism in the late nineteenth and early twentieth centuries. His patents formed the basis of modern alternating current electric power (AC), including polyphase power distribution, and AC motor, crucial for the Second Industrial Revolution. He demonstrated wireless communication (radio) in 1893 and was widely respected as America's greatest electrical engineer (he acquired American citizenship). A unit for measuring magnetic induction (T) was named for him.

Ivan Vučetić (1858–1925)

An anthropologist who invented "dactiloscopy," the science of fingerprinting. He established the first dactiloscopy center in Buenos Aires; Argentine police adopted his method and disseminated it to police forces all over the world.

Rudolf Steiner (1861–1925)

Croatian-born philosopher and writer who founded the Goetheanum, near Basel, and established anthroposophy, a science of human wisdom. Steiner's doctrine of child psychology and learning is the foundation of the Waldorf education system and is practiced in more than eight hundred Waldorf schools around the world.

Dragutin Lerman (1863–1918)

An explorer. A member of Henry Morton Stanley's expedition to the Congo, where he became his most trusted man. Stanley once remarked of him: "The Croat is energetic, cautious, in high spirits."

Slavoljub Euard Penkala (1871–1922)

A Slovak-born engineer and inventor who came to Zagreb and invented the "automatic pencil" (1906). He invented the first solid fountain pen (1907) and started a pen-and-pencil factory that was one of the biggest in the world at that time. His company TOZ-Penkala is still making pens and pencils today.

Ivan Meštrović (1883–1962)

A Croatian sculptor renowned for his religious sculptures, and the first person to have a one-man show at the Metropolitan Museum of Art, New York. In 1927 he entered a design for the coins of the new Irish Free State and, though his proposal arrived after the deadline for consideration, it was actually adopted in 1965 as the seal of the Central Bank of Ireland. He was granted American citizenship by President Eisenhower in person in 1954.

Lavoslav Ružička (1887–1976)

A Nobel Prize winner in Chemistry in 1939 for his work on sex hormones. His laboratory in Zurich became the world center for organic chemistry in prewar times.

Ivo Andrić (1892–1975)

Novelist and short story writer, winner of the Nobel Prize for Literature in 1961.

Antun Augustinčić (1900–79)

Prominent sculptor, whose *Monument of Peace* stands in front of the United Nations building in New York. He taught at L'Ecole des Arts Decoratifs and L'Académie des Beaux-Arts in Paris.

Vladimir Prelog (1906–98)

Nobel Prize winner for Chemistry in 1975 for his works in the field of natural compounds and stereochemistry.

Miljenko Grgić (1923–)

Croatian winemaker who made his career in California. His Chardonnay won first prize at the historic Paris Wine Tasting of 1976, beating French wines that had held primacy till then. His wines are included on the White House wine list.

Goran Ivanišević (1971–)

Former professional tennis player who will be remembered as the only person to win the men's singles title at Wimbledon as a wild card in 2001. His career-high singles ranking was World No. 2 (behind Pete Sampras) in 1994. Ivanišević received the BBC Sports Personality of the Year Overseas Personality Award in 2001.

Goran Višnjić (1972–)

Croatian actor who made his career in the USA. He is best known for his role as Dr. Luka Kovac in the television series *ER*.

Janica Kostelić (1982–)

Considered one of the greatest female skiers of all time. The only woman to win four gold medals in alpine skiing at the Winter Olympic Games in 2002 and

2006, and the only woman to win three alpine Olympic gold medals in one year (2002). She was World Cup champion in 2001, 2003, and 2006. In January 2006 she became only the third woman in World Cup history to win World Cup races in all five disciplines. In 2006 she was awarded Laureus World Sportswoman. Owing to injuries she retired from skiing in April 2007.

Blanka Vlašić (1983–)

The current women's world high-jump champion. Her personal best jump of 6.79 feet (2.07 m) is also the national record, and was set on August 7, 2007, at the World Athletics Championships. Only two women (one indoor and one outdoor) have jumped higher than this.

EXERCISES

Chapter 01 Land & People

❶ Read the following statements and decide whether they are true or false. Write T if the statement is true and F if it is false.

1) There are two climate zones in Croatia: a temperate, continental climate and a pleasant Mediterranean climate. (　　)
2) Split is the center of Dalmatia and the main tourist center on the Croatian coastline. (　　)
3) Under the Emperor Constantine, in the fifth century CE, Croatian territory straddled the border between the Western and Eastern Roman Empire. (　　)
4) The leader of the Party of Rights, Ante Starčević, had the significant role in the awakening of Croatian national spirit. (　　)
5) The Croatian parliament passed a declaration of independence from Yugoslavia on June 25, 1991. (　　)

❷ Answer the following questions in the fewest possible words according to the passage .

1) How many protected national parks are there in Croatia? What are they?
2) How many parts can Dalmatia be divided into? Please write down the parts and their main cities respectively.

★ 答案请到中国外语网（www.cflo.com.cn）“教师资源”板块查询下载。

3) Who was the first Croatian king?

❸ **Think critically and answer the following questions.**

1) Make a brief description on Croatian government.

2) What can you learn from the history of Croatia?

Chapter 02 Values & Attitudes

❶ **Read the following statements and decide whether they are true or false. Write T if the statement is true and F if it is false.**

1) There is no much difference between the younger generation and the older generation in Croatia. (   )

2) The motivation of Croatian identity surviving waves of foreign rulers can be found in the works of Irish writer James Joyce. (   )

3) Due primarily to the support given during the Homeland war, Croats tend to be more open toward Germans than to the British or French. (   )

4) Croatian people place much emphasis on the appearance and the dressing. (   )

5) In Croatia,it is quite obligatory for family members to attend family union in some family festivities such as name days and Church holidays. (   )

❷ **Answer the following questions in the fewest possible words according to the passage.**

1) In what ways do people express their national pride in Croatia?

2) In Croatia, which religion is mostly believed?

3) Where do the Croats love to spend their money?

❸ Think critically and answer the following questions.

1) Please summarize Croats' attitudes toward Serbs.

2) What makes a foreigner be warmly welcomed in Croatia?

Chapter 03 Festivals & Traditions

❶ Complete the sentences with the information given in the passage.

1) Christmas itself begins on (   ), December 24, when families go to (   ).

2) The traditional New Year lunch menu consists of (   ) and (   ).

3) On the first day of Holy Week people go to church with (   ) blessed by priests.

4) Croatian National Day takes place on (   ) every year since 1991.

5) Croatia celebrates All Saint's Day in memory of the martyrs of the (   ) and of (   ).

❷ Answer the following questions in the fewest possible words according to the passage .

1) Which festival has become the first occasion of the year for a mass migration from towns and cities for a short vocation?

2) Which festival is commemorating October 8, 1991?

3) What kinds of wedding ceremony would Croats have?

❸ Think critically and answer the following questions.

1) Does your country have some traditional festivals? How would you describe them?

2) Can you summarize the similarities and differences between Christmas and Spring Festival?

Chapter 04 Making Friends

❶ Read the following statements and decide whether they are true or false. Write T if the statement is true and F if it is false.

1) In Croatian language, *ti* is the formal "you" while *vi* is the informal version. (   )

2) Croats always meet with each other in the bar or the coffee shop. (   )

3) Croats are very talkative and inclined to use body language. (   )

4) In Croatia, sports like football are the most common topic in a conversation. (   )

5) In Croatia,an invitation to someone's home means that a relationship has reached a more intimate plane. (   )

❷ Answer the following questions in the fewest possible words according to the passage .

1) How do neighbors greet and address each other?

2) Where is a good place to meet people?

3) What is the special message when inviting someone for lunch or dinner in a restaurant?

❸ Think critically and answer the following questions.

1) Why can it be difficult for a foreigner to find a social circle in Croatia?
2) Make comments on the way Croats address the senior people in Croatia.

Chapter 05 Daily Life

❶ Complete the sentences with the information given in the passage.

1) The working day for most people is from (　　), until (　　).
2) Croatian children attend at least (　　) —generally language lessons, sports sessions, or drama, ballet, or other dance classes.
3) Croats work on (　　) if they are employed in industry, trade, construction, health services, or similar, and on (　　) if staffing the major shopping centers.
4) In Croatia, housing prices vary depending on the (　　) and the (　　).
5) (　　) is highly developed and widely practiced in terms of taking care of children in Croatia.

❷ Read the following statements and decide whether they are true or false. Write T if the statement is true and F if it is false.

1) Croatian universities have already adopted the European Bologna System. (　　)
2) By the age of eighteen, when secondary school is finished, young Croats can choose either to further their study in university, home or

abroad, or to get a job. (　　)

3) Military service is compulsory for men in Croatia. (　　)

4) Teacher, lawyers and psychologists are greatly needed in Croatia. (　　)

5) Smoking is now prohibited in all public places in Croatia. (　　)

❸ Think critically and answer the following questions.

1) How do Croatia men and women play their role in the family? Make a comparison between Croats and the Chinese counterparts.

2) What is your comment on the after-class measures carried by Croatian primary school?

Chapter 06 Time Out

❶ Choose the most appropriate answer from the four choices according to the information in the passage.

1) Which item in the following is not mentioned as favorite places for Croats to spend their holiday in the passage?

A. Museum.

B. Local coffee shops.

C. Cinema.

D. A weekend house by the sea or in the countryside.

2) Which kind of credit card in the following is accepted in Croatia?

A. American Express.　　B. Master.

C. Visa.　　D. All of the above.

3) Which kind of landscapes cannot be found in Croatia?

A. Continental landscape. B. Mountainous landscape.

C. Xeric landscape. D. Mediterranean landscape.

4) Which cuisine is considered the healthiest in Croatia?

A. Dalmatian cuisine. B. Zagreb cuisine.

C. Istrian cuisine. D. Kvarner cuisine.

5) In Croatia,which kind of dish takes two or three hours to prepare and sometimes has to be ordered in advance with meat and seafood cooked under hot ashes in a casserole dish?

A. *Kulen.* B. *Peka.*

C. *Buzara.* D. *Brodet.*

6) Which wine in the following does not belong to Croatian wine?

A. Marastina. B. Bordeux.

C. Zlahtina. D. Postup.

7) When you are in a restaurant or a coffee shop, it is desirable for you to tip (   ) of the total bill?

A. 5%. B. 8%.

C. 10%. D. 12%.

8) Which kind of sports are most popular in Croatia?

A. Tennis. B. Basketball.

C. Skiing. D. Football.

❷ Think critically and answer the following questions.

1) What are the features of Dalmatian cuisine? What can you learn from it compared to Chinese cuisine?

2) What do you think about tipping?

❶ **Choose the most appropriate answer from the four choices according to the information in the passage.**

1) Visitors from which country need visas if they are staying in Croatia for 80 days?

A. New Zealand. B. Canada.

C. Brazil. D. America.

2) Which item in the following cannot be seen in Croatia?

A. Underground trains. B. Streetcars.

C. Buses. D. Overground trains.

3) Which statement in the following is correct?

A. Croatia has zero tolerance of alcohol on the roads.

B. One cannot use cell phone when driving.

C. One must fasten the belt.

D. All of the above.

4) Where are impossible for travelers to exchange currency?

A. Airport. B. Train station.

C. Department store. D. Bureau de change.

5) Which place in the following are not possible to be adjacent to minefields?

A. Countryside.

B. Main streets in Zagreb.

C. Wastelands on the island of Vis.

D. Beaten track.

❷ Answer the following questions in the fewest possible words according to the passage .

1) In Croatia, when you are ready to travel via Italy, what is your best option?
2) Is there any limitation for residents and nonresidents in Croatia to take into or take out Kuna of the country?
3) Which country has signed a reciprocal agreement with Croatia that enable its passport holders to get free hospital and dental treatment in Croatia?

❸ Think critically and answer the following questions.

1) What kind of transportation will you choose in Croatia, and why?
2) Why can't Croatia's health service meet the standards of the rest Europe or America?

Chapter 08 Business Briefing

❶ Read the following statements and decide whether they are true or false. Write T if the statement is true and F if it is false.

1) It is President Franjo Tudjman that initiated the economic process that led to the alleged "privatization robbery", which enlarges the income disparity. (　　)
2) After the WWII, industry became a dominant element of Croatian economy. (　　)
3) One of the downsides of Croatian business is the excessive paperwork, particularly in the public sector;

4) Trade Unions exist both in the public sector and the private sector in Croatia. (　　)

5) Croats prefer to wear in a Germanic style than in a fashionable yet slightly informal style. (　　)

❷ Answer the following questions in the fewest possible words according to the passage.

1) Which is the mainstay of the tertiary industry in Croatia?

2) What is the World Bank's main concern about Croatia?

3) Which period is a good time for negotiating or finding a job in Croatia?

❸ Think critically and answer the following questions.

1) What kind of features does your presentation need to have if you want to do business with Croats?

2) What is the status quo of trade unions in Croatia? What is your comment?

Chapter 09 Communicating

❶ Read the following statements and decide whether they are true or false. Write T if the statement is true and F if it is false.

1) The oldest document in the Croatian language is the Vinodol Code. (　　)

2) It is impolite in Croatia to stand close to each other when in a conversation. (　　)

3) Among over two hundred radio stations, state-owned HR1 and HR2

broadcast politics, news, sports, and entertainment in Croatia. (　　)

4) Post offices also handle telegrams, faxes, utility bills, and currency exchange all in one counter in Croatia. (　　)

5) Optima Telecom is one of the Internet providers in Croatia. (　　)

❷ Answer the following questions in the fewest possible words according to the passage .

1) When was the first Croatian grammar published?

2) What does it mean when people join their thumb and forefinger to form a circle?

3) Which is the biggest telephone company in Croatia?

❸ Think critically and answer the following questions.

1) Summarize the development of Croatian language.

2) Why is body language useful?